THE VOCABULARY BUILDER WORKBOOK

burnish • avatar • intemperate
• thespian • raconteur • obstrepe
ppelganger • horology • susurru
pariah • wanderlust • dilettante
• gratuitous • preamble • parochi
sure • filial • tumultuous • perfu
torturous • raillery • calumny •
raduce • litigious • beguile • imp
• propitiate • phantasmagorical
orripilation • prodigious • raille
arduous • tumultuous • perfunc
• moribund • chrysalis • forensic
iposte • incontrovertible • susu
g • debauchery • bucolic • peren
erminable • horology • tumultuo
cataclysm • hamper • pastoral •
• immemorial • desultory • usur
rouse • intimate • propitiate • s
lum • intemperate • crepuscula
stultifying • buoyant • cogent •

THE VOCABULARY BUILDER WORKBOOK

SIMPLE LESSONS AND ACTIVITIES
TO TEACH YOURSELF OVER
1,400 MUST-KNOW WORDS

CHRIS LELE from Mag**oo**sh

ZEPHYROS
PRESS

For general information on our other products and services or to obtain technical support, please contact our Customer Care Department within the U.S. at (866) 744-2665, or outside the U.S. at (510) 253-0500.

Zephyros Press publishes its books in a variety of electronic and print formats. Some content that appears in print may not be available in electronic books, and vice versa.

TRADEMARKS: Zephyros Press and the Zephyros Press logo are trademarks or registered trademarks of Callisto Media Inc. and/or its affiliates, in the United States and other countries, and may not be used without written permission. All other trademarks are the property of their respective owners. Zephyros Press is not associated with any product or vendor mentioned in this book.

ISBN: Print 978-1-93975-481-3 | eBook 978-1-93975-482-0

To my Dad, for showing me the power of words.

CONTENTS *(n.)* kən'tents

burnish • avatar • intemperate
• thespian • raconteur • obstrepe
ppelganger • horology • susurru
pariah • wanderlust • dilettante
• gratuitous • preamble • parochi
sure • filial • tumultuous • perfu
torturous • raillery • calumny
traduce • litigious • beguile • imp
• propitiate • phantasmagorical
orripilation • prodigious • raille
arduous • tumultuous • perfunct
• moribund • chrysalis • forensic
riposte • incontrovertible • susu
g • debauchery • bucolic • peren
erminable • horology • tumultuo
cataclysm • hamper • pastoral •
• immemorial • desultory • usurr
grouse • intimate • propitiate • s
lum • intemperate • crepuscula
stultifying • buoyant • cogent • d

INTRODUCTION

People tend to assume I've always excelled at words. I'm a decent Scrabble player, include SAT words in conversation without realizing it, and do anagrams in my head for fun. Now that I'm a "vocabulary expert" at Magoosh, my innate verbal ability seems like a foregone conclusion.

But it wasn't always this way. When I was in middle school, I remember having to study for vocabulary quizzes and dreading the experience. To make matters worse, my father would get excited every time he saw me with the vocabulary book open. "Ask me any word," he'd exclaim. No matter how many syllables the word contained, he'd toss off definitions with aplomb, pressing me for another, the way a small child might ask for candy. I assumed he'd always known such words, and that this knowledge came easily to him. Meanwhile, I would be condemned to uttering no more than three-syllable words—and to poor grades on vocabulary quizzes.

I redoubled my efforts at studying, and while my quiz scores did inch up slightly, I felt that my father existed on some vocabulary plane that I'd never attain. What I didn't realize then was that my father's level of knowledge was very much within my grasp, but not from trying to memorize lists of words in a vocabulary book. For that's all our school gave us: books containing lists of words, with no exercises or examples providing context, just dry definitions to be parroted back for a passing grade.

As I grew older, I became an avid reader. First I tried to figure out words in context and then always (and I mean *always*) consulted the dictionary. Now the previously dry, boring definition contained a special resonance: It unlocked the meaning of a word I had encountered "in the wild." And learning words begot more words. Soon, I was actively seeking to grow my vocabulary, picking up books that would offer vivid example sentences, colorful descriptions of a word's history, and synonyms galore. While providing riveting reading material (at least for a word lover), these books typically did not contain exercises to reinforce what I learned. It was only through sheer time and effort that I was able to build a strong vocabulary.

What I hope to give to you, the reader, is a book that extends beyond mere examples of words in sentences and word history—however colorful—and allows you to engage in activities that reinforce the words you've studied. Using this book, you will learn not merely to parrot a definition but to understand how a word functions in context. That way, you won't only recognize words—you'll be able to use them yourself. By the time you've completed the lessons and activities in this book, you'll be a testament to what took me many years to realize: A large vocabulary is not built from memorizing word lists or from some innate verbal capacity that very few possess, but rather is formed through targeted practice and context recognition.

HOW TO USE THIS BOOK

This book is divided into 200 lessons, each featuring six to eight words that fit into the lesson's category. To test your knowledge of many of the words just introduced, you'll find a short activity at the end of each lesson asking you to use the new vocabulary in matching, unscrambling, and fill-in-the-blanks exercises.

Many lessons have been created by grouping words according to a theme that presents words along a spectrum. For instance, Lesson 17's theme is "Only Fools Rush In," which includes words that mean "careful" and "thoughtful," in addition to words that mean "careless" and "reckless." This means that the words featured in each lesson are typically not all synonyms, as that would limit the range of possible activities—as well as make for dull reading. Additionally, this spectrum allows us to explore the sometimes-subtle distinctions between words.

There is no single best way to use this book, as each of us has different needs. For instance, you might want to start by learning word roots if your vocabulary is not very strong. I find that learning roots is helpful for beginning students of vocabulary, because it allows them to group similar words around a small and thus easier to memorize segment of that word. At the other end of the spectrum, you might already have a strong vocabulary and wonder what in this book will be of value to you. To challenge even the word mavens among us, I have included some very difficult (though not too obscure) words. So as not to alienate beginner and intermediate learners, the words are arranged within each lesson according to difficulty.

Each lesson begins with three words, arranged in order from easiest to most difficult. For each I offer the part of speech, pronunciation, definition, an example of the word in a sentence, etymology (or word history), and finally an interesting tidbit to keep in mind. For the remaining four or five words in the lesson, I provide only the part of speech, pronunciation, and definition. These words are also arranged from simplest to most advanced. The last word of this group is usually a tough one. Indeed, sometimes the final two words are both pretty recondite (yes, that word is included in this book!). The words are followed by an activity to help you gauge your understanding.

So, if you're a beginner, you might want to focus on just a few words per lesson and then try the activity at the end. Intermediate learners might want to attempt the entire lesson. Finally, those who already have a strong vocabulary can just skim the hardest words in each lesson.

That said, I do encourage everyone to try the activities, since their purpose is to reinforce what you've learned. Merely reading a definition and thinking "I've got it" isn't the same as actually testing yourself.

Finally, don't assume that by reading this book one lesson at a time, without ever going back to previous sections, you'll retain very much. A vocabulary book, after all, is not a novel. Make a habit of revisiting previous lessons and redoing the activities (you might want to jot your answers on a separate piece of paper). After all, it is better to obtain a strong sense of a quarter of the words in this book than a tenuous grasp of half.

One last point: You should use this book in conjunction with reading. And I don't mean just any reading. Seek out newspapers such as the *New York Times* or magazines such as the *New Yorker* or the *Atlantic*. As you read the articles in these publications, you'll recognize many of the words featured in this book. When we encounter words in their "natural habitat," not only do we get a deeper understanding of how they're used, but that encounter will be unexpected, making it more likely that our brains will retain the information. Ultimately, that is the intention of this book: to make us better readers, better writers, and better thinkers.

FOR PARENTS AND TEACHERS

Setting Expectations

The pace at which readers should progress through this book is determined to a large extent by the literacy level of the student. A good test of whether students should move on to another lesson is to ask them the definition of three words chosen at random from about 25 words (about three lessons). If they are able to tell you at least two definitions, then it is likely that they are ready to progress. Of course, watch out for "parrots," those who recite a definition perfectly but can't effectively use the word in a sentence. For this group, having them come up with an original sentence using the word is a good test of comprehension.

If a student is retaining at least 60 percent of the words they learn, three lessons per week is a good pace. However, you might want to slow down the pace to two lessons a week to make sure the student is learning vocabulary cumulatively and not just scoring B or A on the weekly quiz and then forgetting most of the words a few weeks later.

A few signs that a student should slow down:

- Merely parrots definitions

- Forgets most of the words from the previous week

- Is unable to provide definitions for two out of three words chosen at random from three lessons

- Seems to know the definitions but struggles with the fill-in-the-blank questions

A few signs that a student should speed up:

- Already knows many of the words in the lesson

- Provides definitions to three out of three words chosen at random from three lessons

Motivating Students

Some students may become bored, thinking that if they answer most of the activity questions correctly they are done learning. The key to improving one's vocabulary is to commit words to long-term memory, so with these students, it is essential to continue testing them by choosing words at random. You might want to read fill-in-the-blank sentences out loud to see if they can come up with the word on their own.

For those students who easily become discouraged, it's important to emphasize quality over quantity. Give them time to spend with just a few words and encourage them to use any of the additional resources mentioned in this book to provide them with deeper context of how a word is used. You might also give them tools such as flashcards to help them commit words to long-term memory. Additionally, they should be encouraged to use these words in the "real world"—that is, to relate them to something in their lives—so the words don't slip from their minds after a few days (see "Out and About" below).

Out and About

New words are all around us—from what we read online and in books to what we hear in the news and from our friends and colleagues. Looking up words that you don't know is an excellent habit that should be encouraged. And with so many of us wielding smartphones these days, checking definitions has never been easier.

But the more real-life associations we can make with new words, the better. The truth is that students going through this book will have plenty of words swimming around in their heads. By thinking that those words are relevant only when they open up this vocabulary book, the student is missing out on a rich opportunity: to use these words in daily life.

Encourage students to engage in one or more of these activities:

1. Use three words you learned that day as you walk to school.

2. Use some of the words you've learned in this book to describe the latest TV show you watched.

3. Use new words to describe whatever your mood happens to be.

4. Choose words from this book to describe five people you encounter throughout the day—though you might want to keep the word to yourself!

5. If you know the student has a specific interest or hobby, find an article relating to that. Have them read the article, and then quiz them on any relevant vocabulary afterward.

Measuring Progress

It is important to gauge just how much information a student is retaining. Yet, if they do poorly on a vocabulary quiz, they are likely to lose motivation. After all, one of the worst outcomes would be a student walking away from this book believing they're "just not a vocabulary person," when the real culprit was too many words thrown at them at once. Or perhaps the fact that they didn't understand some definitions but were too afraid to say so.

So measuring progress is important, because it can reveal whether we need to slow down. It can also show us whether a student is flourishing. The key is to do it often, but in small doses. In other words, it is more effective to quiz a student on two or three lessons before moving on, rather than wait till they've worked through ten lessons only to find out that they are hardly retaining anything.

So how do we know if they are actually learning from the book?

- They are able to score well on quizzes in which they have to not just define a word but also demonstrate how it is used.

- They are able to make connections with other words that are synonyms or antonyms, whether those words are in the same lesson or a previous one.

- They are able to come up with part of the word, if before they were struggling to come up with anything at all.

- You hear them use a word as a part of normal conversation.

Finally, learning vocabulary takes a lot of commitment, and some students might be tempted to give up. But the more committed you are, the more that will inspire them to keep up with it. If you show joy at using these words (and even learning a few new ones yourself), that passion for learning will be contagious.

PRONUNCIATION GUIDE

a	cat, flap		**o**	lock, dot
ā	page, face		**ō**	lobe, snow
ä	far		**ô**	lord, board
b	bar, cab		**oi**	boy, soil
CH	check, catch		**ou**	cow, doubt
d	doll, bad		**o͝o**	full, book
e	pet, best		**o͞o**	ghoul, boo
ē	eat, bee		**p**	part, trap
er	germ, earn		**r**	run, start
f	fear, leaf		**s**	sell, rest
g	grow, leg		**SH**	bash, flush
h	her, hand		**t**	tire, great
i	itch, tin		**TH**	thump, path
ī	idle, wire		**Ө**	them, breathe
j	joke, giraffe		**v**	vest, cove
k	key, rock		**w**	word, wilt
l	low, ball		**y**	yum, yell
m	man, ram		**z**	zoo, graze
n	nose, run		**ZH**	measure, vision
NG	sing, wrong		**ə**	as in the *a* in *alert* or the *e* in *taken*

Parentheses indicate that the word can also be pronounced without the syllable enclosed in the parentheses.

An accent on top indicates that stress should be put on the following syllable. An accent at the bottom indicates that stress should be placed on the previous syllable.

THE LESSONS

Prefix: *Pre-* (PART 1)

Pre- is the Latin root meaning "before," so it serves as a perfect place to begin this book—a kind of prelude.

preamble *(n.)* prē͵ambəl
An introduction to a text.

*The most recognized **preamble**—the beginning of the United States Constitution—was written by Thomas Jefferson.*

This comes from the Latin for "walking before"; the Latin verb *ambulare* means "to walk." The word *preface* is a common synonym, though it usually refers to an introduction to a book, whereas *preamble* refers to an introduction to a formal document.

presage *(v.)* presij
To indicate something (usually bad) is about to happen.

*The sudden loss of jobs **presaged** an economic downturn.*

The Latin word *ōmen* is thought to be the origin for *presage*. *Presage* can also be a noun, describing an incident or event that presages something.

prescient *(adj.)* preSH(ē)ənt
Having knowledge of something before it happens.

*Kevin was so **prescient**—predicting the winners of the last five World Series—that his friends joked he was psychic.*

Scient comes from a root meaning "to know." The less common *nescient* plays on the same root (*ne-* meaning "not") and describes somebody who is ignorant.

predilection *(n.)*
predl'ekSHən
A special fondness.

precipitate *(adj.)*
prəˈsipətət
Rash, acting without thinking.

predicate *(v.)* ˈpredəkāt
To be based on.

presentiment *(n.)*
prəˈzentəmənt
A feeling that something (typically bad) is about to happen.

ACTIVITY 1

Write the word that completes each sentence:

1. He was known to be _____, once rushing out of his house without his shoes.

2. She had a _____ for small, quiet cafés, where she could sit and read undisturbed.

Mark "S" if the meanings of the two words are similiar, "R" if they are related, or "NR" if they are not related:

3. prescient and presage _____

4. preamble and predicate _____

Prefix: *Pre-* (PART 2)

precedent *(n.)* ˈpresədənt
Something that sets an example for how things are done in the future.

*The teacher told the student that if she let him turn in his homework late, it would set a **precedent** for the rest of the class to do the same.*

Precedent is closely related to *precede*, which means "to go before." Another closely related word is *unprecedented*, meaning that something is unlike anything that has come before it.

pretentious *(adj.)* prəˈtenSHəs
Acting more important than others by pretending to know more.

*After returning from Europe, Dwight behaved in a **pretentious** way, speaking with a foreign accent and telling all his friends they had no idea what they were missing.*

This word is related to *pretend*. *Pretentious* always has a negative connotation, unlike its antonym, *unpretentious*, which is generally positive.

pretense *(n.)* prēˌtens
A claim or assertion not based on fact.

*He finally dropped the **pretense** that everything was fine and began listing his complaints.*

Pretense is derived from the Latin verb *praetendere* meaning to "allege in excuse" or "extend in front," though the current meaning has diverged from this. *Pretense* is closely related to *pretentious*, both of which are related to *pretend*.

predecessor *(n.)*
ˈpredəˌsesər
One that comes before, often a person who previously held a position before passing it on to someone else.

precursor *(n.)* prēˈkərsər
Something that comes before another; used only for things, not for people.

pretext *(n.)* prēˌtekst
A reason given for something that is not the actual reason.

precocious *(adj.)*
prəˈkōSHəs
Developing early (usually in terms of ability).

preclude *(v.)* prəˈklo͞od
To make it impossible for something to happen.

ACTIVITY 2

Write the word that completes each sentence:

1. The five-year-old was clearly _____, able to play Vivaldi's *The Four Seasons* by ear.

2. A felony record can _____ employment at many companies.

3. The fire was without _____: Never in the state's history had 50 percent of its forest burned down.

Mark "S" if the meanings of the two words are similiar, "R" if they are related, or "NR" if they are not related:

4. precursor and predecessor _____

5. pretense and precedent _____

6. pretext and precocious _____

Eponymous Parts of Speech from Antiquity (PART 1)

Eponyms are words that are derived, or taken, from the name of a person, place, or thing either real or fictional.

tantalize (*v.*) tan(t)lˌīz
To torment someone with something they want without ever giving it to them.

*The photos of white sand beaches he hung in his office merely **tantalized** Robert; he never could find time for a vacation.*

Tantalus was a mythological figure who spent eternity grasping for a fruit that was just outside his reach. Tantalus also stood in a pool of water that receded every time he tried to take a drink.

pyrrhic (*adj.*) pirik
Describing a victory that comes with a heavy cost.

*Becoming the citywide spelling bee champ was a **pyrrhic** victory for Shannon; she spent so much time studying that she had few friends.*

Pyrrhus was a Greek general triumphant in battle, but at such great cost that he was unable to continue fighting the Romans. *Pyrrhic* is almost always followed by the word *victory*.

laconic (*adj.*) ləˈkänik
Using as few words as possible when speaking.

*Hollywood often portrays cowboys as **laconic** types, who mutter no more than a few syllables as replies.*

Laconia was a region in ancient Sparta, where its inhabitants were known for using few words. Philip of Macedon is said to have told the Spartans, "If I attack your land, I will utterly destroy it." The reply was simply: "If."

draconian (*adj.*)
drəˈkōnēən
Extremely strict, as laws or rules.

jeremiad (*n.*) jerəˈmīəd
A long speech full of complaints.

cicerone (*n.*) sisəˈrōnē
A guide who gives speeches to sightseers.

ACTIVITY 3

Match the word with its meaning:

1. laconic _____
2. jeremiad _____
3. cicerone _____
4. draconian _____
5. pyrrhic _____
6. tantalize _____

a. a guide who gives speeches to sightseers

b. describing a victory that comes with a heavy cost

c. to torment someone with something they want without ever giving it to them

d. extremely strict, as laws or rules

e. a long speech full of complaints

f. using as few words as possible when speaking

Eponymous Parts of Speech from Antiquity (PART 2)

nemesis *(n.)* neməsəs
One who constantly works to ensure another's downfall.

*No matter how well Greg played soccer, his **nemesis**, the fleet-footed Betty, always outplayed him.*

Nemesis was the god of anger, known for his great vengeance. Most comic book characters have a nemesis; for instance, Batman has the Joker, while Superman has Lex Luthor.

platonic *(adj.)* pləˈtänik
Describes a close relationship that has no romantic or sexual basis.

*The two had a **platonic** relationship, sharing gourmet recipes, works of literature, and classical music CDs.*

Platonic is derived from Plato, the philosopher known for his great mind. Another way of looking at *platonic* is that it describes the absence of any romance.

thespian *(n.)* THespēən
An actor.

*Rita was quite the **thespian**, acting in all of her school's plays.*

According to legend, Thespis was the first actor in ancient Greece. This word is usually used in a sarcastic sense.

spartan *(adj.)* spärtn
Lacking in comfort or flourishes (describing either a lifestyle or accommodations).

juggernaut *(n.)* jəgərˌnôt
An unstoppable, destructive force or thing.

maudlin *(adj.)* môdlən
Overly self-pitying, often used to describe someone who becomes sentimental when intoxicated.

hector *(v.)* hektər
To bully (usually through words).

ACTIVITY 4

Unscramble the word and define:

1. p a n s t a r _____

2. p o n t i c a l _____

3. p i e s t h a n _____

4. e t o r c h _____

Write the words that complete the paragraph:

Though the home team was able to stop their _____, their opponent's star player was a true _____, slam-dunking over everyone. Yet, in the end, it was a _____ victory. Their all-state point guard broke his collarbone, and after losing the last three games of the year, the team was _____, lapsing into bouts of self-pity.

Words from French (PART 1)

French has given us a surprising array of English words, everything from *restaurant* to *denim*. Pay careful attention to the pronunciation of these words as they may differ significantly from what you expect.

nonchalant *(adj.)* nänSHəˈlänt
Giving off a sense of calmness and coolness.

*Katy lulled opponents by **nonchalantly** walking onto the court; only when the whistle blew did she explode with ferocity.*

Nonchalant is derived from a French word meaning "indifferent," or "not caring." *Nonchalant* is synonymous with *insouciant* (see sidebar) and is much more commonly used.

adroit *(adj.)* əˈdroit
Skillful, either mentally or with one's hands.

*She was a master networker, **adroit** at shifting conversations from one person to another.*

Adroit is from the French *à droit*, meaning "according to right" or "properly." Good synonyms to know are *adept* and *dexterous* (used only for manual adroitness). Alternatively, the word *maladroit* means "clumsy."

chicanery *(n.)* SHəˈkān(ə)rē
Trickery or deception, usually in politics or where money is involved.

*The mayor was known for his **chicanery**, over the years cheating the public out of millions.*

Chicanery comes from a French verb meaning "to trick." Good synonyms to know are *duplicity* and *subterfuge*, which also describe kinds of deception.

demur *(v.)* dəˈmər
To object to doing something.

insouciant *(adj.)* inˈso͞osēənt, inˈso͞oSHənt
Showing a lack of concern or interest.

arriviste *(n.)* ärēˈvēst
A person who is extremely ambitious and has recently acquired wealth or power.

parvenu *(n.)* pärvəˌn(y)o͞o
A person who has recently gained status or celebrity.

ACTIVITY 5

Match the word with its synonym:

1. arriviste   chicanery

2. insouciant   parvenu

3. subterfuge   nonchalant

Write the word that completes each sentence:

4. Carl didn't find the two-hour walk too difficult, but he wanted to _____ the next morning when his friends proposed a strenuous hike.

5. The new senator easily beat out his predecessor, who was known for his _____.

Words from French (PART 2)

rapport *(n.)* raˈpôr, rəˈpôr
Understanding and similar feelings that exist between people or groups.

*Sarah took no time at all in establishing a **rapport** with others, talking to strangers on the train platform as though they were long-lost friends.*

Rapport comes from an Old French word for "relationship" and "harmony." This word is similar to "mutual understanding," but always implies a friendly relationship.

passé *(adj.)* paˈsā
No longer in fashion.

*Over the years her style has become **passé**—after all, who wears pastels these days?*

From the French for "past, gone by." Google shows that the word *passé* is itself becoming somewhat *passé*, its use dropping since 1900.

cache *(n.)* kaSH
A collection of items hidden or stored away for future use.

*The bears had discovered the campers' food **cache**, making away with everything from sugar-coated cereal to beef jerky.*

From the French for "to hide," *cache* was often used by French Canadian hunters to describe where they hid their provisions. *Cache* has also come to mean "short-term computer memory where information is stored for easy retrieval."

raconteur *(n.)* räˌkänˈtər
A skilled storyteller.

sortie *(n.)* sôrˈtē
An attack from a defensive position.

gauche *(adj.)* gōSH
Clumsy and socially awkward.

sangfroid *(n.)* säNGˈfrwä
Utter calmness and composure, especially under pressure.

ACTIVITY 6

Write the word that completes each sentence:

1. Nobody had ever stood up to the intimidating principal before, but with complete _____, Alice listed what was wrong with the cafeteria menu.

2. The two baseball coaches had a good _____ and chatted animatedly on the field before their teams faced off.

3. Larry had not shopped for clothes in nearly five years, during which time most of the styles he favored had become _____.

Provide the word for the given definition:

4. clumsy and socially awkward = _____

5. a collection of items hidden or stored away for future use = _____

6. a skilled storyteller = _____

Words from French (PART 3)

liaison (*n.*) lēə͵zän, lēˈāzän
A person who helps two parties communicate.

*The prime minister was wary of meeting foreign dignitaries, so he used his trusted advisor as a **liaison**.*

Originally a cooking term, meaning "to bind together." *Dangerous Liaisons* is an Oscar-winning film from 1988 that depicts the scheming of the French royal court.

envoy (*n.*) ˈän͵voi
A messenger, usually on a diplomatic mission.

*During medieval times, being an **envoy** was a perilous job, given the constant threats from bandits.*

From the French for "one sent." On the other hand, an *envoi* (note spelling) is a type of poem.

sans (*prep.*) sanz
Typically a facetious way of saying "without."

*A roundabout way of saying naked is "**sans** clothing."*

From Old French, meaning "without." The sans-culottes were lower-class revolutionaries during the French Revolution. Culottes were breeches, or short pants, fashionable with the upper classes; the sans-culottes favored longer pants.

filial (*adj.*) filyəl
Relating to the obligations of a son or daughter.

droll (*adj.*) drōl
Odd and therefore amusing.

ACTIVITY 7

Fill in the missing letters to complete each word and then define it:

1. _ i _ i s _ n _____

2. s _ _ s _____

3. _ r o _ _ _____

4. _ n v o _ _____

5. _ i _ i a _ _____

Compound Words and Phrases from French

French also gives us many phrases, composed of two or more words, that have been integrated into English. Add these to your conversation to give a little dash of sophistication.

faux pas *(n.)* fō-ˈpä
An act or comment with embarrassing social consequences.

The diplomat quickly lost his overseas post after one too many faux pas.

This is French for "false step." Though we often hear it used in the phrase *fashion faux pas*, the term can apply to any social blunder. It is spelled the same in the singular and the plural.

in lieu of *(prep.)* in loo əv
In place of, substitute.

A good online dictionary can be used in lieu of a traditional desktop dictionary.

Lieu is the French word for "place." The word *lieu* is not typically used by itself in English.

enfant terrible *(n.)* änfän teˈrēbl(ə)
A person whose commentary or behavior is aimed to shock.

Lady Gaga, the pop music artist, was seen by many as an enfant terrible for wearing a dress made out of meat during the MTV music awards.

In French this word translates literally to "terrible child." Note that the plural of *enfant terrible* is *enfants terribles,* with an *-s* on the ends of both words.

tête-à-tête *(n.)* tetəˈtet
A private conversation between two people.

savoir vivre *(n.)*
savwär veevruh
A familiarity and ease with polite society.

savoir faire *(n.)*
savwär ˈfer
The skill of saying and doing just the right thing in social situations.

esprit de corps *(n.)*
eˌsprē də ˈkôr
The spirit of belongingness and pride of a tightly knit group.

ACTIVITY 8

Match the phrase to its meaning:

1. in lieu of _____
2. savoir vivre _____
3. savoir faire _____
4. tête-à-tête _____
5. enfant terrible _____
6. esprit de corps _____
7. faux pas _____

a. a familiarity and ease with polite society
b. a person whose comments or behavior is aimed to shock
c. the spirit of belongingness and pride of a tightly knit group
d. an act or comment with embarrassing social consequences
e. in place of
f. a private conversation
g. the skill of saying and doing just the right thing

Words from German

Jawohl! German has contributed more to English than you might realize. Below are some Germanic words, both common and challenging.

poltergeist *(n.)* pōltər͵gīst
A ghost that supposedly causes noisy disturbances in the environment.

*Though home alone, Mark and Lisa heard the sound of crashing dishes from downstairs; Mark shrugged and said, "**Poltergeist.**"*

This translates literally to "noisy ghost." Those who saw the early 1980s film *Poltergeist* will find this an easy word to remember.

kitsch *(n.)* kiCH
Cheap art whose owners are usually aware of its lack of value.

*Greta's house was full of **kitsch**: amateur sketches of sunsets, plastic trinkets, and unidentifiable items she'd picked up at a bazaar.*

Comes from the German for "trash." The adjective *kitschy* is also commonly used.

doppelganger *(n.)* däpəl͵gaNGər
A person who looks remarkably like another person.

*Many believe that each one of us has a **doppelganger** walking around, a virtual twin.*

In German this means "double goer." An eerie version of a doppelganger involves the singer Justin Timberlake and a Civil War veteran who looks exactly like him.

kaput *(adj.)* kəˈpo͞ot
No longer functioning, as a device or machine.

verboten *(adj.)* fərˈbōtən, vərˈbōtən
Forbidden or prohibited.

zeitgeist *(n.)* tsīt͵gīst
The mood of a particular time period as captured by ideas and culture.

schadenfreude *(n.)* SHädən͵froidə
Delight taken in another's misfortune.

bildungsroman *(n.)* bildo͞oNGzrō͵män
A coming-of-age story.

ACTIVITY 9

Provide the word for the given definition:

1. a ghost that supposedly causes noisy disturbances = _____

2. forbidden or prohibited = _____

3. the mood of a particular time period as captured by ideas and culture = _____

4. delight in another's misfortune = _____

5. a coming-of-age story = _____

6. no longer functioning, as a device or machine = _____

7. cheap art whose owners are usually aware of its lack of value = _____

8. a person who looks remarkably like another person = _____

Words with an Italian Origin (PART 1)

While many words derive from Latin, to which Italian is closely related, some words come to us directly from Italian.

citadel *(n.)* sitədəl
A fortress standing above and protecting a city.

*Once the **citadel** had fallen to the marauders, the residents lost hope of defending their city.*

This comes from an Old Italian word for "city."

burlesque *(n.)* bərˈlesk
An exaggerated imitation of something, typically in a dramatic work.

*The Monty Python comedy team has done a hilarious **burlesque** on the search for the Holy Grail.*

Burlesque is originally from the Italian for "ludicrous," but has come more recently from French. *Burlesque* can also refer to a variety show, typically for adults.

pastiche *(n.)* paˈstēSH
A mixture of elements that typically don't go together.

*The television show was a **pastiche** of 1970s sitcoms and 1980s science-fictional dramas.*

This comes from the Italian for "paste," but like *burlesque*, is more recently from French. A pastiche can also refer to a musical work composed completely of ideas taken from different works.

archipelago *(n.)*
ärkəˈpeləˌgō
A cluster of islands.

salvo *(n.)* salˌvō
A simultaneous discharge of guns, often used figuratively to mean a verbal attack.

imbroglio *(n.)* imˈbrōlyō
A complicated (and embarrassing) situation or mess.

littoral *(adj.)* lidərəl
Located along the shoreline.

ACTIVITY 10

Write the word that completes each sentence:

1. The Greek _____ is a popular destination for those who enjoy island hopping.

2. Overlooking the city was a mighty _____ that few would ever consider attacking.

3. The artist's musical style is a _____ of jazz, hip-hop, and electronica.

4. Things seemed to have died down between the two feuding celebrities until one of them unleashed a _____ on social media.

Provide the definition:

5. littoral = _____

6. imbroglio = _____

7. burlesque = _____

Words with an Italian Origin (PART 2)

bravado *(n.)* brəˈväˌdō
A bold act meant to show off.

The teenage boys jumped into the water from increasingly higher points on the rock, but their bravado did not impress the girls below.

Related to the sixteenth-century Italian word for "brag," this word can also be traced to Middle French and Spanish. Notice that the root *brav-* is very similar to "brave."

manifesto *(n.)* manəˈfestō
A document describing the aims of a group or organization.

The political splinter group first became known when it posted a 50-page manifesto in the city park, asking that the current government step down because of years of corruption.

From the Italian for "a public declaration." Karl Marx's *The Communist Manifesto* is one of the best-known manifestos in history.

ruffian *(n.)* rəfēən
A person inclined to violence and criminal behavior.

The town had become much safer, compared to the early days when ruffians would prowl the street looking for victims.

This word comes from both Old French and Italian and describes a pimp or, more generally, anyone willing to commit a crime. Think of this word as a combination of *bully* and *criminal*. (Notice, as well, that "ruff-" sounds exactly like "rough.")

dilettante *(n.)* diləˈtänt
Someone who develops an interest in an area of art or music without being a true expert.

cognoscenti *(n.)*
känyəˈSHentē
Those who are well versed in a particular subject.

intelligentsia *(n.)*
inˌteləˈjen(t)sēə
The intellectuals or highly educated people in a society.

ACTIVITY 11

Write the words that complete each sentence:

1. Gloria was no _____; she had been a staff writer for an art magazine and was considered one of the _____ in the subject of chiaroscuro.

2. When the _____ walked by, Stefan, in an act of _____, yelled, "Keep on walking, buddy!"

Provide the definition:

3. intelligentsia = _____

4. manifesto = _____

Words from India

Surprisingly, Hindi and Sanskrit, the ancient Indian languages, have given us such common terms as *pajamas* and *shampoo*. Here are some other words that may sound familiar but whose exact definition eludes you.

guru *(n.)* go͞oro͞o
One who is a master in his or her field.

*Eli hired a self-proclaimed tech **guru** to fix his laptop, but his computer still would not reboot.*

Originally from Hindi for "learned teacher." *Guru* can also refer to a spiritual teacher, especially in Hinduism or Buddhism.

bungalow *(n.)* bəNGgə͵lō
A low, one-story house, usually with a large porch or veranda.

*The family would retreat to their country **bungalow**, where they'd enjoy long Sunday afternoons sipping tea on the veranda.*

This word derives from the Indian state Bengal, where this type of home was originally found. Traditional bungalows in India had a thatched roof, typically made of straw.

pundit *(n.)* pəndət
An expert in a specific field.

*The president's controversial Supreme Court pick will have all the television networks trotting out their favorite **pundits** come morning.*

Sanskrit, an ancient language of India, is the source of *pundit*, which means "learned master." Though *pundit* and *guru* are very similar, today a *pundit* most often refers to an expert in a field (usually politics) who offers up his or her opinion, whereas a *guru* simply describes an expert.

karma *(n.)* kärmə
In Hinduism and Buddhism, the determination of one's fate by one's actions.

mantra *(n.)* mantrə
An oft-repeated phrase or slogan.

avatar *(n.)* avə͵tär
The embodiment of a certain idea in a person.

pariah *(n.)* pəˈrīə
An outcast.

ACTIVITY 12

Match the word with its meaning:

1. a low, one-story house, usually with a large porch or veranda _____

2. an expert in a specific field _____

3. the determination of one's fate by one's actions _____

4. an outcast _____

5. an oft-repeated phrase or slogan _____

6. the embodiment of a certain idea in a person _____

7. a master _____

a. pundit

b. pariah

c. mantra

d. avatar

e. bungalow

f. karma

g. guru

Traveling Words

Now that we've "traveled" to a few different countries by looking at some of the words they've contributed to English, it makes sense to explore terms that relate to travel itself—or, in some cases, the lack of travel.

wanderlust *(n.)* wändər͵ləst
A strong and constant desire to travel.

*Felix spent his twenties trying to satisfy his **wanderlust**, visiting no fewer than 50 countries on four continents.*

Wanderlust comes from the German for "desire for wandering." *Wanderlust* is also the name of a British magazine that describes itself as "for people with a passion for travel."

cosmopolitan *(adj.)* käzmə'pälətən
Comfortable and familiar with many different cultures.

*She became much more **cosmopolitan** after a dozen trips abroad, achieving near fluency in Spanish and French.*

The origin of *cosmopolitan* is the Greek words *kosmos* ("world") and *politēs* ("citizen"). You can think of someone who is cosmopolitan as a citizen of the world.

insular *(adj.)* ins(y)ələr
Closed off from the rest of the world, unfamiliar with other cultures.

*Since the dictator had closed off the country from foreign influence, the populace was becoming more **insular** with each passing year.*

From the Latin for "belonging to an island." *Insular* is an antonym of *cosmopolitan*.

provincial *(adj.)*
prə'vin(t)SH(ə)l
Narrow-minded, unexposed to different cultures or ideas.

jaunt *(n.)* jônt
A journey taken for pleasure.

parochial *(adj.)* pə'rōkēəl
Having a narrow or limited perspective.

junket *(n.)* jəNGkət
An extravagant trip, usually funded by the government or some other entity.

ACTIVITY 13

Mark "S" if the meanings of the two words are similar, "O" if they are opposite, or "D" if they are different:

1. cosmopolitan and insular _____

2. provincial and parochial _____

3. jaunt and junket _____

4. wanderlust and parochial _____

Misleading Words (PART 1)

Much of this book features lessons based on roots, from both Latin and Greek. However, you'll find that some words appear to have familiar roots but actually mean something completely different. This is either because that root has taken on a different meaning in a particular word, or because it is in fact a different root entirely.

sedulous *(adj.)* sejələs
Hardworking and attentive.

*The father **sedulously** painted each of the small toy trains before presenting them to his son.*

While this word might remind you of *sedentary*, it has a different Latin root, meaning "busy" or "diligent." Think of *sedulous* as a combination of *diligent* and *detail-oriented*.

restive *(adj.)* restiv
Restless, agitated.

*The citizens became **restive** in the wake of the earthquake, their supplies dwindling and little relief on the horizon.*

Though this word might sound like *restful*, it signifies the exact opposite. *Unruly* and *uncontrollable* are two synonyms for *restive*.

peruse *(v.)* pəˈro͞oz
To read carefully.

*It is always advisable to **peruse** legal documents.*

Peruse can also mean "to glance over or through in a casual manner." Synonyms for *peruse* include *scrutinize* and *inspect*.

punctilious *(adj.)*
pəNG(k)ˈtilēəs
Extremely careful about details, to the point of being fussy.

equivocate *(v.)*
əˈkwivəˌkāt
To be intentionally vague and misleading.

predicament *(n.)*
prəˈdikəmənt
A difficult situation that isn't easy to escape.

prepossessing *(adj.)*
prēpəˈzesiNG
Attractive and charming.

ACTIVITY 14

Provide the word for the given definition:

1. a difficult situation that isn't easy to escape = _____

2. attractive and charming = _____

3. extremely careful about details, to the point of being fussy = _____

4. restless, agitated = _____

5. hardworking and attentive = _____

6. to read carefully = _____

7. to be intentionally vague and misleading = _____

Misleading Words (PART 2)

gratuitous *(adj.)* grəˈt(y)o͞oətəs
Unwarranted or uncalled for, given the situation.

*Kevin decided to boycott the spelling bee, claiming it was **gratuitous** to have to repeat the word after saying it once and correctly spelling it.*

Many think of *gratuity*—from the restaurant bill—when they see this word, or even link it with *grateful* or *gratitude*. *Gratuitous* can also describe a service provided for free. However, this usage is much more uncommon.

intemperate *(adj.)* inˈtemp(ə)rət
Given to excess, typically with regard to drinking alcohol.

*Even those counting calories can become **intemperate** during the holiday season.*

Though this word seems to relate to one's mood or temper, it actually refers to one's appetite. The opposite of this word—*temperate*—gave its name to the Temperance movement, a period during which alcohol was banned in America.

burnish *(v.)* bərniSH
To make shiny.

*Karen spent the entire afternoon **burnishing** the silver until she could see her reflection perfectly.*

This word does not relate to setting anything on fire. Rather, it comes from an Old French word meaning "to polish." This word can also be used figuratively to describe the process of polishing something to improve one's image, for example a resume.

quiescent *(adj.)* kwēˈesnt
Describing a state or period of inactivity.

redress *(v.)* rəˈdres
To make right or correct some wrongdoing.

remiss *(adj.)* rəˈmis
Negligent, derelict, lackadaisical, or neglectful.

preeminent *(adj.)* prēˈemənənt
The best of its kind.

mannerism *(n.)* manəˌrizəm
A way of speaking or behaving that is specific to an individual.

ACTIVITY 15

Write the word that completes each sentence:

1. As much as the prime minister hoped the publicity would _____ his dwindling reputation, the country saw through his motives.

2. Hoping to _____ the fact that he cut in line, he explained that he was late to pick up his son at school.

3. The parking attendant was _____ in his duties due to his habit of napping during his shift.

4. After months of ominous rumbling, the volcano has thankfully become _____.

5. Derrick's _____ days were over, and he gave up alcohol entirely.

6. She felt that her brother's high fives were _____ because even when she didn't do a good job, there was his hand.

Quiet to Noisy

These words range from the calm and serene to the loud and out of control.

placid *(adj.)* plasəd
Tranquil, calm.

*As Bucky neared 12 years old, his formerly feisty nature disappeared, and he became **placid**, hanging out on the porch and wagging his tail.*

Placid comes from a Latin word meaning "to please." You might know this word from Lake Placid, a lake that is, by all accounts, peaceful.

rambunctious *(adj.)* ramˈbəNG(k)SHəs
Out of control and overly excited.

*The **rambunctious** trio of toddlers bounced about the room, oblivious to the adults whispering "shush."*

This word likely came from a similar old word, *rumbustious*. Synonyms are *boisterous* and *unruly*.

susurrus *(n.)* sōōˈsərəs
A whispering or rustling sound.

*The late autumn wind made itself known in the **susurrus** of freshly swept leaves.*

This comes from the Latin meaning "to whisper." Given this word's poetic flair, it tends to appear mostly in literary contexts.

murmur *(v.)* mərmər
To say very softly, almost indiscernibly.

raucous *(adj.)* rôkəs
Loud and unruly.

hubbub *(n.)* həbəb
The loud noise caused by a crowd.

obstreperous *(adj.)* əbˈstrepərəs
Very noisy and out of control.

ACTIVITY 16

Give three words that mean the opposite of *placid* (the first letters are given):

1. r_____

2. r_____

3. o_____

Write the word that completes each sentence:

4. The new student tended to _____ when he spoke, so the teacher had to strain to hear him.

5. From a mile away, the waterfall was a mere _____, its violent power not yet manifest.

6. Because of the _____ of her office party, Patricia could barely hear the voice on her phone.

Only Fools Rush In

There are a host of words in English that mean "to rush in without thinking." There are also a few that express the exact opposite.

prudent *(adj.)* pro͞odənt
Careful and thoughtful.

*The squirrel is known for being **prudent**, storing acorns away for later rather than eating them all at once.*

This word comes from a Latin word for *provident*, meaning "to foresee and make provision for the future." Good synonyms to know are *judicious* and *discreet*. On the other hand, the opposite of *prudent* is *imprudent*.

wary *(adj.)* werē
Cautious and alert.

*The hikers had heard reports of a grizzly bear, so they were **wary** as they stepped through the dense forest.*

Wary derives from an Old Norse word for "attentive." A good way to think of this word is "on the lookout" or "on one's toes."

impetuous *(adj.)* imˈpeCH(o͞o)əs
Acting without forethought, reckless.

*The young lovers were so **impetuous** that they ignored their parents' warnings and eloped under the cover of night.*

Comes from a Middle English word meaning "violent." The noun form, *impetuosity*, is not commonly used these days, but there's a good chance you'll stumble upon it in the works of Jane Austen.

heedless *(adj.)* hēdləs
Reckless.

chary *(adj.)* CHerē
Careful and cautious.

rash *(adj.)* raSH
Acting without thinking.

ACTIVITY 17

Mark "S" if the meanings of the two words are similar, "O" if they are opposite, or "D" if they are different:

1. heedless and chary _____

2. impetuous and rash _____

3. prudent and wary _____

Speaking Words

Many English words mean "talkative," while others mean "quiet."

reticent *(adj.)* retəsənt
Tight-lipped, not offering one's thoughts freely.

*The suspect was **reticent**, wary that he might reveal something that could be used against him in court.*

The origin of *reticent* is a Latin word meaning "to be silent." *Reticent* is a popular word on the SAT and GRE.

garrulous *(adj.)* ger(y)ələs
Speaking more than necessary, chatty.

*While many faulted Nate for being **garrulous**, it was just his way of building rapport.*

This word comes from the Latin for "throat" (to remember *garrulous*, think of the word "gargle," which involves your throat, as does speaking). This word is a synonym of *loquacious*.

verbose *(adj.)* vərˈbōs
Using more words than necessary.

*Patrick tended to be **verbose**; he believed that the more he talked, the more his personality would shine through.*

Comes from the Latin meaning "full of words." Whereas *garrulous* refers only to speech, *verbose* can also be used to describe writing. In this context, two good antonyms to know are *succinct* and *concise*.

taciturn *(adj.)* tasəˌtərn
Quiet and reserved, brooding.

mince *(v.)* mins
To not speak directly for fear of offending.

hedge *(v.)* hej
To not commit oneself fully verbally.

loquacious *(adj.)* lōˈkwāSHəs
Talkative, long-winded.

palaver *(n.)* pəˈlavər
Idle chatter.

ACTIVITY 18

Provide the word for the given definition:

1. using more words than are necessary = _____

2. idle chatter = _____

3. to not speak directly for fear of offending = _____

4. to not commit oneself fully verbally = _____

5. quiet and reserved = _____

Just How Much? (PART 1)

Quantity words abound in English, such as the word *abound* itself. Here are some important ones to know.

cornucopia *(n.)* kôrn(y)əˈkōpēə
A large supply of something desirable.

*The weekend spa retreat offered a **cornucopia** of indulgences, everything from a two-hour massage to energy healing.*

Comes from the "horn of plenty," a legendary horn capable of conjuring up whatever its owner desired.

legion *(adj.)* lējən
Large in number.

*Though her detractors are **legion**, the pop singer still sells millions of copies of each of her albums.*

This word historically described a large group of Roman soldiers, but today it can refer to any multitude. *Legion* can also be a noun referring to any large group, often of people; good synonyms for the noun form are *throng* and *horde.*

surfeit *(n.)* sərfət
Too much of something.

*There is a **surfeit** of online news sources, though most tend to fall on one side or the other of the political spectrum.*

Surfeit is from the French verb *faire* meaning "to do" and *sur-* meaning "over." This word is often used in the context of food and drink, which is not surprising given that one of its older meanings was "overindulgence."

glut *(n.)* glət
An excess.

multitude *(n.)*
məltəˌt(y)ōod
A great number.

myriad *(n.)* mirēəd
An immense number.

plethora *(n.)* pleTHərə
An excessive number of something.

copious *(adj.)* kōpēəs
Abundant in number.

ACTIVITY 19

Write the word for each etymology or "root history."

1. horn of plenty = _____

2. "to overdo" in French = _____

3. large group of Roman soldiers = _____

Unscramble the word and define:

4. dairym _____

5. hareplot _____

Just How Much? (PART 2)

paucity *(n.)* pôsətē
Lack of something.

*Citizens claim that there has been a **paucity** of goodwill, with few reaching out to help in a time of need.*

Originally from the Latin for "a few." Another way of saying paucity is *scarcity* or *lack*.

superfluous *(adj.)* so͞oˈpərflo͞oəs
Excessive, nonessential.

*He had already notified his friends via text that he would be late for the movie, so he figured that posting an additional message on social media would be **superfluous**.*

Another word that comes from Latin, this one meaning *super-* ("over") and *fluous* ("flow").

wanting *(adj.)* wän(t)iNG
Lacking, deficient.

*Jerry's charm was clearly **wanting**, yet he still wondered why his dates never went well.*

This word comes from Old Norse for "deficiency."

dearth *(n.)* dərTH
Lack, scarcity.

modicum *(n.)* mädəkəm
A limited quantity.

iota *(n.)* īˈōtə
An extremely small amount.

extraneous *(adj.)*
ikˈstrānēəs
Nonessential.

ACTIVITY 20

Provide the word for the given definition:

1. excessive, nonessential = _____

2. a limited quantity = _____

3. an extremely small amount = _____

4. lacking = _____

5. lack (two words) = _____

In My Opinion

Humans are an opinionated bunch, and we have vocabulary that does an excellent job of capturing this.

dogmatic *(adj.)* dôg'madik
Claiming one's opinion as though it were the unarguable truth.

*William became **dogmatic** in his insistence on the superiority of his wine, stating its many excellent attributes, even though we all found it undrinkable.*

This word comes from the Greek *dogma*, meaning "a fixed belief." Another way to think of dogmatic is "highly opinionated."

didactic *(adj.)* dī'daktik
Trying to instruct or impart knowledge, but typically in a way that is slightly condescending.

*Heather's attention began to wander as the lecturer became increasingly **didactic** about the difference between a semicolon and a comma.*

Also from Greek, but this time from a word meaning "to teach." An *autodidact* is somebody who is self-taught. This relatively uncommon word does not carry a negative connotation.

retract *(v.)* rə'trakt
To take back a statement or an offer.

*Once video footage revealed that she had accidentally scratched her own car, she **retracted** the statements she'd made earlier about my careless driving.*

From the Latin for "to draw back." *Forswear* is a synonym, along with *deny*.

assertive *(adj.)* ə'sərdiv
Willing to advocate for oneself, confident.

repudiate *(v.)* rə'pyo͞odē͟ āt
To reject, to renounce.

adamant *(adj.)* adəmənt
Unyielding, not giving in.

doctrinaire *(adj.)* däktrə'ner
Sticking to a fixed way of doing something despite changes in circumstances.

ACTIVITY 21

Write the word that completes each sentence:

1. He enjoyed teaching others whenever he could, though his friends found him _____.

2. Though he was seen at the scene of the crime, the defendant continued to _____ any charges to the contrary.

3. Even though the situation had changed drastically, John was _____, insisting that his friends follow the original plan.

4. Despite the fact that the so-called UFO had revealed itself to be nothing more than a distant cloud, the six-year-old was _____ that she had witnessed a flying saucer.

5. The mother encouraged her son to be more _____, to speak up for himself when he felt others were taking advantage of him.

How Big Is Your Appetite?

English has a healthy selection of words for "very hungry" and also a bunch for those who deny themselves even the smallest of pleasures.

voracious *(adj.)* vəˈrāSHəs
Having an extremely large appetite.

*A **voracious** eater, Mark ploughed through a mountain of food that summer.*

From the Latin for "large appetite;" notice the similarity between *vor-* and *-vour*. The word can also be used figuratively.

ascetic *(adj.)* əˈsetik
Denying oneself simple pleasures, typically for religious reasons.

*As soon as January rolled around, Trevor became **ascetic**, eating only small servings of rice and chicken for 30 days.*

Originally used to describe Christians who went to the desert to live in seclusion with very few means. Be careful not to confuse this word with *aesthetic*, which means "pertaining to beauty."

abstemious *(adj.)* əbˈstēmēəs
Refraining from drinking or eating too much.

*In an effort to be kind to his liver, Harold became **abstemious**, drastically cutting his vodka intake.*

Temetum is the Latin for "intoxicating drink," while *ab-* is a root meaning "away." This word is not as extreme as *ascetic* and also applies only to food and drink, and not lifestyle.

insatiable *(adj.)*
inˈsāSHəb(ə)l
Describing a hunger that cannot be satisfied.

sate *(v.)* ˈsāt
To satisfy in terms of consuming enough.

gourmand *(n.)* go͝orˈmänd
Person who enjoys fine food, typically to excess.

ravenous *(adj.)* rav(ə)nəs
Extremely hungry, insatiable.

ACTIVITY 22

Mark "T" for true and "F" for false:

1. someone who is ascetic is also abstemious _____

2. someone who is easily sated is insatiable _____

3. a gourmand tends to be ravenous _____

4. someone who is voracious isn't easily sated _____

A Question of Trust

While some words for trust exist, they seem to be outnumbered by those for deceit.

hoodwink *(v.)* hŏŏdˌwiNGk
To deceive.

The Internet is awash in various schemes that try to **hoodwink** *you into coughing up your credit card info.*

Comes from the sixteenth century and means "to blind by covering the eyes." A less common synonym is *cozen*, which implies clever trickery.

charlatan *(n.)* SHärlədən
Someone who pretends to have knowledge they don't to hoodwink you.

"Fake it till you make it" is the credo of the **charlatan**, *who will try to pass off phony knowledge.*

Originates from Old Italian for "to babble." The movie *Catch Me If You Can* is the true tale of Frank Abagnale, who was the consummate charlatan, pretending at various points in his life to be a doctor, a pilot, and a lawyer.

steadfast *(adj.)* stedˌfast
Firmly devoted.

Throughout life, Patrick could count only a few **steadfast** *friends, those who had kept by his side even during the most trying times.*

From the Old English for "standing securely in place." *Staunch* and *dedicated* are two synonyms for *steadfast*.

bilk *(v.)* bilk
To cheat or swindle, usually involving money.

ruse *(n.)* rōōz
A clever trick.

bamboozle *(v.)*
bamˈbōōzəl
To cheat or deceive.

stalwart *(adj.)* stôlwərt
Loyal and reliable.

fidelity *(n.)* fəˈdelədē
Faithfulness, loyalty.

ACTIVITY 23

Match the word with its definition:

1. charlatan _____

2. bilk _____

3. ruse _____

4. fidelity _____

5. hoodwink _____

a. a trick

b. faithfulness, loyalty

c. to deceive

d. someone who pretends to have knowledge they don't actually possess

e. to cheat or swindle, usually involving money

Is That a Compliment? (PART 1)

Whether compliment or insult, we have plenty of words in English to convey the exact sentiment.

laud *(v.)* lôd
To praise for great work, typically in public.

*He was **lauded** in the city newspaper for his years of volunteer work.*

Laud comes from Latin, meaning "commend, honor, praise." *Acclaim* and *commend* are two synonyms.

lionize *(v.)* lī̇ə͵nīz
To treat as a celebrity.

*In certain parts of the country, some hometowns **lionize** their high school teams and players the way they would professional athletes.*

This word comes from England, by way of the Tower of London. Centuries ago, lions were kept in the Tower of London as an object of curiosity, drawing droves of spectators.

deprecate *(v.)* deprə͵kāt
To express disapproval.

*Mario typically **deprecated** romantic comedies, but (much to his dismay) he found himself laughing at the movie his wife dragged him along to see.*

From the Latin for "praying against one deemed evil." A similar word is *depreciate*, which means "to lower in value."

derisory *(adj.)*
də ˈrīs(ə)rē
Derisive, putting down someone or something.

hail *(v.)* hāl
To praise or acclaim, usually loudly.

approbative *(adj.)*
uh-proh-buh-tiv
Expressing approval.

reproach *(v.)* rə ˈprōCH
To express disappointment.

ACTIVITY 24

Complete the word for each definition:

1. to treat like a celebrity = __ioni__

2. to express disappointment = rep_____

3. to praise publicly = l___d

4. to acclaim vigorously = __ai__

5. to express disapproval = de_____ate

6. expressing approval = __ ro__tive

Is That a Compliment? (PART 2)

slight *(v.)* slīt
To insult by ignoring.

*Jeremy intended to **slight** Mark by not inviting him to his bachelor party.*

This comes from a word meaning "to have little worth." The common definition of this word—"small in physical stature"—comes from a different root word, meaning "smooth."

pejorative *(adj.)* pəˈjôrədiv
Describing a word or phrase that has a negative association.

The word garbage man *has a **pejorative** ring to it, and has in the last few decades been replaced by the term* sanitation worker.

Derived from the Latin for "to make worse." *Pejorative* can also be a noun denoting a word with a negative connotation.

kudos *(n.)* k(y)o͞oˌdäs
Praise given for a job well done.

*Every Friday, the company encouraged a round of **kudos**, in which each employee praised a fellow coworker for something they had done well during the week.*

Kudos originally came from a Greek word used to express praise or glory or success on the battlefield. This word is often used informally to mean "congratulations."

venerate *(v.)* venəˌrāt
To respect deeply.

belittle *(v.)* bəˈlidl
To insult, put down.

commend *(v.)* kəˈmend
To praise.

revere *(v.)* rəˈvir
To respect deeply.

ACTIVITY 25

Provide the word for the given definition or etymology:

1. the opposite of *complimentary* = _____

2. from the Latin for "to worship" (hint: it's not *revere*) = _____

3. sounds like it has to do with size and means "to insult" = _____

4. a praising word from ancient Greek = _____

5. to applaud or praise = _____

From Lazy to Lively

The next time you feel your energy fading, use some of these words to spice things up, rather than just saying, "I'm tired."

phlegmatic *(adj.)* fleg'madik
Apathetic, unemotional.

On the morning of the SAT, the students walked into the classroom, one phlegmatic face after another.

The bodily humor *phlegm* is the source of this word. The ancients believed that if you were too full of phlegm, you would feel sluggish. This word sometimes has a negative association.

indolence *(n.)* indələnts
Laziness.

The summer months bred indolence in the city folk, with few setting foot outdoors unless it was really necessary.

Dole comes from the Latin root for "pain," and *in-* means "without." *Indolent* is the adjective form; *lethargic* and *languid* are two common synonyms.

vivacious *(adj.)* və'vāSHəs
Lively and animated.

She was vivacious one moment, lethargic the next, so quickly had the sedative taken effect.

From the Latin for "long-lived, vigorous." *Vivace* is one of the fastest tempos in music.

alacrity *(n.)* ə'lakrədē
Cheerful promptness in response.

torpid *(adj.)* tôrpəd
Sluggish, lethargic.

ebullient *(n.)* i'bo͞olyənt
Highly and vigorously enthusiastic.

exuberant *(n.)* ig'zo͞ob(ə)rənt
Highly enthusiastic.

ACTIVITY 26

Mark "S" if the meanings of the two words are similar, "O" if they are opposite, or "D" if they are different:

1. torpid and ebullient _____

2. alacrity and indolence _____

3. vivacious and phlegmatic _____

4. exuberant and ebullient _____

Hard at Work?

Whether you are hard at work on this book or not, one of the following words will likely describe you.

industrious *(adj.)* in'dəstrēəs
Hard-working and diligent.

Most of the new hires were **industrious,** *working till well past 7 p.m.*

This word comes from Latin for "diligence." The noun form—*industry*—can also mean "hard work."

lackadaisical *(adj.)* lakə'dāzək(ə)l
Lazy and unenthusiastic.

The new recruits were so **lackadaisical** *that most of them didn't make it past the first week of boot camp.*

Lackaday, short for *alack the day,* was an expression used to express sorrow in the 1590s.

feckless *(adj.)* fekləs
Unmotivated, incompetent, irresponsible.

Many of the **feckless** *youth who had once gathered outside the mall were now grown up and working inside, some with great industry.*

This comes from the Scottish word *feck,* which is a shortening of the word *effect.* One who is feckless, then, doesn't have much effect. The word *feck* never quite took off in the United States.

bustle *(v.)* bəsəl
To move about actively.

dispatch *(n.)* də'spaCH
Speed at completing a task.

celerity *(n.)* sə'lerədē
Swiftness.

assiduous *(adj.)* ə'sijo͞oəs
Working painstakingly to get a job done.

ACTIVITY 27

Write the word that completes each sentence:

1. With the end of the quarter approaching and one last chance to hit their sales goals, the telemarketers were even more _____ than usual.

2. On the last day before vacation, the employees _____ about the office looking busy but not actually getting anything done.

3. The messenger moved with _____, hoping to deliver the telegram on time.

4. Jonas was _____, and his attitude toward many things could be summed up by one word: blah.

Words About Words (PART 1)

In this self-reflective lesson, we examine the potential of words themselves.

palindrome *(n.)* palən͵drōm
A word or phrase that reads the same forward as it does backward, such as *radar* and *kayak*.

*The sentence "Go hang a salami, I'm a lasagna hog" is a **palindrome**.*

From the Greek, *palin-* means "again/back" and *dromos* means "running."

portmanteau *(n.)* pôrtˈmantō
A word formed by parts of two other distinct words, such as *smog*, which consists of the *sm* from *smoke* + the *og* from *fog*.

*The word "electrocution" is a little-known **portmanteau**—a mash-up of the words "electricity" and "execution."*

The French verb *porter* ("to carry") and noun *manteau* ("mantle") refer to a suitcase consisting of two compartments. The simpler term for portmanteau words is "blend."

brunch *(n.)* brən(t)SH
A late-morning meal that has elements of both breakfast and lunch.

*A delicious **brunch** is served at the new restaurant.*

Brunch is a portmanteau of *breakfast* and *lunch* (*br* from breakfast + *unch* from lunch).

neologism *(n.)* nēˈälə͵jizəm
A new word or expression.

In the 1990s the word Internet *was a **neologism**, though these days the term seems as though it has been around forever.*

From the root *neo-* for "new" and *logos-* for "word." *Chillax* and *staycation* are twenty-first-century neologisms that also happen to be portmanteaus.

archaic *(adj.)* ärˈkāik
Describing a very old word, typically no longer in use.

barbarism *(n.)*
bärbə͵rizəm
A word that does not obey the rules of written language.

tautology *(n.)* tôˈtäləjē
A redundancy, essentially saying that A equals A.

eponymous *(n.)*
əˈpänəməs
Named after a person.

ACTIVITY 28

Write the word that matches each example:

1. it's the right thing to do, because the right thing is what we'll do _____

2. ain't _____

3. describing a sixteenth-century word no longer in use _____

4. the island of Victoria is named for the queen _____

5. racecar and rotor _____

6. this book is a real vocabathon _____

Words About Words (PART 2)

bombastic *(adj.)* bämˈbastik
Describing someone whose speech is inflated and self-important.

*The school superintendent carried on in his normal **bombastic** manner, puffing out his chest and intoning how each student was extremely privileged to belong to a historic and noble tradition.*

From the Old French for speech that is inflated and self-important. *Fustian*, a synonym—albeit an uncommon one—was also used to describe a type of cotton.

cryptic *(adj.)* kriptik
Intentionally vague or mysterious.

*When his friends asked if he'd visit while they were studying abroad, he answered **cryptically**, "You never know."*

From *kryptikos*, the Greek for "hidden." Though thesauruses list *enigmatic* and *cryptic* as synonyms, *enigmatic* simply means "mysterious" without the connotation of any intentional motive.

turgid *(adj.)* tərjəd
Describing writing that is bombastic and puffed up.

*The manager wrote long, **turgid** emails that contained little substance but conveyed to the recipient the manager's sense of self-importance.*

This word comes from the Latin for "to swell." *Turgid* can also describe physical swelling, as of body parts.

lucid *(adj.)* lo͞osəd
Clear and easy to understand.

oblique *(adj.)* əˈblēk
Indirect (describing communication).

limpid *(adj.)* limpid
Very clear and easy to understand (referring to writing).

sesquipedalian *(n.)* seskwəpəˈdālyən
A person inclined to using very long words.

ACTIVITY 29

Mark "S" if the meanings of the two words are similar, "O" if they are opposite, or "D" if they are different:

1. lucid and limpid _____

2. turgid and cryptic _____

3. bombastic and oblique _____

4. sesquipedalian and limpid _____

Where Did You Go to School?

A range of words exists to describe levels of education and knowledge one might possess. Here are a few good ones to know.

pedantic *(adj.)* pəˈdan(t)ik
Overly fussy in one's concern for trivial academic knowledge.

"Actually, the Battle of Hastings happened in the eleventh century," *was a typical interjection of my* **pedantic** *friend Sebastian.*

This word comes from the Latin for "teacher."

erudite *(adj.)* er(y)əˌdīt
Displaying scholarly knowledge.

The professor fit the **erudite** *part well: a book of poetry in his tweed jacket pocket and a pair of thick glasses set low on the bridge of his nose.*

From the Latin for "to instruct." *Erudite* has a positive connotation, whereas *pedantic* has a negative one.

pedagogue *(n.)* pedəˌgäg
A teacher, typically a strict one.

Mr. Harris was a true **pedagogue,** *giving copious amounts of homework and never accepting a late assignment.*

Pedagogue comes from the Greek for "boy" and "guide." Today, *pedagogue* can refer to a teacher of both boys and girls.

unlettered *(adj.)*
ənˈledərd
Illiterate.

benighted *(adj.)* bəˈnīdəd
Unenlightened.

collegial *(adj.)* kəˈlēj(ē)əl
Describing a warm chumminess between a group of associated people.

eminent *(adj.)* emənənt
Prominent, distinguished.

ACTIVITY 30

Write the word that completes the sentence:

1. Mr. Ellis was more _____ than _____, since he had memorized a bunch of obscure facts that did not truly indicate deep learning.

2. The _____ scholar was appointed chairman of the recently founded archeological society.

3. The principal had had enough administrative work and found himself back in the classroom in the role of _____.

4. The atmosphere among the engineering team was _____; everyone had a shared sense of purpose and was always eager to help others.

5. Under the repressive regime, the populace had remained _____, totally out of touch with the rest of the world.

Mind Your Manners

Behaving properly is important. But for those of us who choose not to, there are plenty of words to use.

churlish *(adj.)* CHərliSH
Intentionally rude.

*The man was habitually **churlish** and enjoyed driving slowly in the fast lane just to watch people's reactions.*

This comes from Old English to describe a peasant. A *churl* is a noun describing one who is rude and lacks manners.

indiscreet *(adj.)* indəˈskrēt
Drawing attention to actions or behavior that should remain private.

*Most people are not so **indiscreet** as to mention their digestive issues at the dinner table—then there's Bob.*

This comes from a Latin word meaning "indistinguishable." One who is discreet is careful not to draw attention to such actions. These days, people often say "TMI," meaning "too much information." This is usually a sign that the person sharing this information is being indiscreet.

idiosyncrasy *(n.)* i-dē-ə-ˈsin-krə-sē
A peculiar characteristic or temperament.

*Steve Jobs was known as a man with many an **idiosyncrasy**—but his peculiarities were indivisible from his genius.*

This word is a splendid mixture of a number of Greek roots, essentially meaning "one's own personal blending."

etiquette *(n.)* edəkət
Proper behavior and conduct.

brusque *(adj.)* brəsk
Short and to the point in a way that is considered rude.

irascible *(adj.)* iˈrasəb(ə)l
Easily angered.

impolitic *(adj.)* imˈpälə.tik
Unwise.

ACTIVITY 31

Mark "S" if the meanings of the two words are similar, "R" if they are related, or "NR" if they are not related:

1. idiosyncrasy and mannerism _____

2. churlish and indiscreet _____

3. brusque and impolitic _____

4. etiquette and irascible _____

Is It Clear?

Some concepts are easy to understand. Others are recondite—like that very word.

inscrutable *(adj.)* inˈskro͞odəb(ə)l
Difficult, if not impossible, to understand.

Though the text was billed as an introduction to physics, it was **inscrutable** *to all but those with a physics degree.*

The *scrut-* comes from the Latin for "to search." The *in-* negates this root. This word is related to *scrutinize*, which means to examine carefully.

esoteric *(adj.)* esəˈterik
Describing knowledge that is intended for only a specific few.

Tax codes can seem downright **esoteric** *unless you've spent years studying the jargon.*

Comes from a Greek word meaning "part of the inner circle." This word not only refers to academic or intellectual pursuits but also to everyday things—for example, "Her meals are unique because she uses esoteric spices."

currency *(n.)* kərənsē
General use, acceptance, or prevalence.

The notion that Pluto is no longer a planet still does not have **currency** *in some circles.*

This comes from the Latin word for *current* (think flowing water) and was later used by John Locke to describe the flow of money. *Currency* has two distinct meanings, one which relates to money and the other which relates to how commonly accepted or used something is.

abstruse *(adj.)* abˈstro͞os
Abstract and difficult to grasp.

pellucid *(adj.)* pəˈlo͞osəd
Extremely clear.

recondite *(adj.)* rekənˌdīt
Too obscure and deep to understand.

arcane *(adj.)* ärˈkān
Known by only a few.

ACTIVITY 32

Mark "S" if the meanings of the two words are similar, "O" if they are opposite, or "D" if they are different:

1. abstruse and pellucid _____

2. recondite and arcane _____

3. currency and esoteric _____

4. inscrutable and esoteric _____

Words Describing Character

While these words aren't necessarily the most complimentary, they might describe someone you know.

philistine *(n.)* filəˌstēn
A person who is hostile toward arts and culture.

*Paul was an outright **philistine**, claiming that looking at paintings is a waste of time.*

In the Old Testament, this word refers to the people of Philistia, who were enemies of the Israelites. A confrontation in the sixteenth century between university students and townspeople had the former describing the latter as lacking in culture and civilization, alluding to the biblical Philistines.

ignoble *(adj.)* igˈnōbəl
Having a dishonorable character.

*The villain was so **ignoble** that even though he owed his life to the heroine, he schemed to bring about her downfall.*

Comes from the French meaning "not honorable." *Despicable* and *dastardly* are two good synonyms.

base *(adj.)* bās
Contemptible, low-minded.

*When the defendant revealed that he had committed the crime solely for the money, the jury viewed his motive as **base** and ultimately found him guilty.*

This word is similar to the French word *bas*, which means "low." In this case, *low* refers to one's morals.

contemptible *(adj.)*
kənˈtem(p)təb(ə)l
Despicable.

vulgar *(adj.)* vəlgər
Common in a cheap, tasteless way.

wayward *(adj.)* wāwərd
Difficult to control.

uncultivated *(adj.)*
ənˈkəltəˌvādəd
Lacking education or refinement.

ACTIVITY 33

Write the word that completes each sentence:

1. He was not surprised that others called him a _____—after all, he thought classical music was purely for snobs.

2. Those who knew him knew he was no angel, yet they were surprised at what a _____ thing he had done. (3 possible answers)

3. The way in which the family flaunted their inheritance was _____—did anyone really need to own three Bentleys?

4. His taste in fashion was _____: A baggy sweater over gym shorts and tube socks was his usual attire.

Musical Words

Music has given us some words that can apply to a broader context. Some important ones are presented here.

crescendo (*n.*) krəˈSHenˌdō
A gradual increase, or the point of greatest intensity or climax.

Her resentment toward the governor reached a **crescendo** *by midsummer, at which point she stepped down from her office.*

From the Italian for "increase," this word describes a musical passage that gets increasingly louder.

coda (*n.*) kōdə
The concluding part of something.

The **coda** *to the esteemed director's career was a 15-minute compilation of highlights from his many beloved films.*

The Italian for "tail" is the source of this word, and describes the last section of a composition, often musical.

mellifluous (*adj.*) məˈliflo͞oəs
Sweet sounding.

The middle movements of Mozart's piano concertos offer themes so **mellifluous** *that it is easy to see why many regard him as divinely blessed.*

From the Latin for "flowing like honey," this word doesn't have a direct musical reference, though it usually refers to something very pleasant sounding.

forte (*adj.*) ˈfôrˌtā, fôrt
Loud in music.
(*n.*)
An area in which one excels (the noun version doesn't just broaden the definition [the way that *crescendo* does] but leads to a different use of the word)

amplify (*v.*) ampləˌfī
Increase the volume, get louder.

virtuoso (*n.*)
vərCHəˈwōsō
A person very accomplished at a musical instrument.

ACTIVITY 34

Write the word that completes each sentence:

1. Vladimir Horowitz is regarded as the foremost piano _____ of the twentieth century, able to play much of the classical repertoire with great emotional depth.

2. Music was never his _____, though he was gifted at painting.

3. The soprano's _____ voice enraptured the crowd.

4. As the deadline approached, the anxious chatter rose to a _____.

5. The once-celebrated actor had an unfortunate _____ to his career, being arrested numerous times.

Animal Words

The animal kingdom has bestowed on us a large collection of descriptive vocabulary—words with meanings that often hark back to some physical trait or characteristic of various animals.

dogged *(adj.)* dôgəd
Persistent, even in the face of adversity.

*Had the detective not been so **dogged**, she would have likely missed the one extremely subtle clue that eventually broke the case wide open.*

In the 1300s, this word related to one of the more negative qualities of dogs. This word can be used both negatively (somebody doesn't know when to give up) or positively (somebody doesn't give up despite adversity).

mulish *(adj.)* myo͞oliSH
Stubborn, obstinate.

*Jimmy becomes **mulish** as soon as his mother asks him to do any chores.*

Relating to a mule, which is the offspring of a donkey and a horse.

badger *(v.)* bajər
To harass and pester.

*Though Phyllis told her little brother he couldn't have the chocolate bar until the weekend, he continued to **badger** her about it.*

Possibly from Middle High German and French, meaning "badge" and "bold." This word is different from the others in this lesson because it refers to another animal. In this case, dogs were used to try to get a badger out of a cage, a low entertainment of the time.

ape *(v.)* āp
To imitate.

crow *(v.)* krō
To gloat loudly.

slothful *(adj.)* ˈslôTHfəl
Lazy.

waspish *(adj.)* wäspiSH
Easily angered.

ACTIVITY 35

Provide the word for the given definition:

1. to harass and pester = _____

2. to imitate = _____

3. to gloat loudly = _____

4. lazy = _____

5. stubborn = _____

Words Describing Animals

In the previous lesson, we looked at some words with animals at their roots. Here we present a range of adjectives that describe specific types of animal.

bovine *(adj.)* bōvīn
Describing a person who is slow and unintelligent.

*Each morning Hal would shuffle around his kitchen with a **bovine** expression on his face—until he had his morning coffee and snapped to life.*

From the Latin for "ox" or "cow." The bovine family includes not only cows, but also oxen, bison, sheep, buffalo, and goats.

vulpine *(adj.)* vəlˌpīn
Cleverly deceitful.

*The German general Erwin Rommel was **vulpine** indeed, outsmarting Allied commanders for years and earning the sobriquet "Desert Fox."*

From the Latin *vulpinus*, meaning "fox."

elephantine *(adj.)* eləˈfan(t)ēn
Enormous, massive.

*This unabridged dictionary is **elephantine** on two counts: It weighs over 20 pounds and contains over 100,000 words.*

From the Greek *elephantinos*.

simian *(adj.)* simēən
Relating to apes.

ursine *(adj.)* ərˌsin
Relating to bears.

apian *(adj.)* ˈāpēən
Relating to bees.

avian *(adj.)* ˈāvēən
Relating to birds.

asinine *(adj.)* asəˌnīn
Describing a donkey; slow-witted.

ACTIVITY 36

Match the animal to its adjective:

1.	elephant	avian
2.	bee	asinine
3.	ape	bovine
4.	fox	ursine
5.	donkey	vulpine
6.	bird	apian
7.	bear	elephantine
8.	cow	simian

Religious Words (PART 1)

These words are strongly connected to the Christian church but can also apply to a broader context—rather than being purely *sacerdotal*, which means "relating to priests."

apostate *(n.)* əˈpäˌstāt
A person who rejects or abandons a strongly held belief.

In increasing numbers, on both the political left and right, **apostates** *have come to label themselves as "centrists" or "independents."*

This word comes from the Greek for "a runaway slave." The noun form, *apostasy*, is also common.

sanctimonious *(adj.)* saNG(k)təˈmōnēəs
Pretending to be religious and holy, but doing so as a pretext to look down on others.

The inquisitor pointed at the condemned and gave them a **sanctimonious** *lecture about the importance of faith.*

From the Latin meaning "holy in character." *Holier-than-thou* is an informal way of saying *sanctimonious*.

iconoclast *(n.)* īˈkänəˌklast
One who defies convention in a striking fashion.

Jackson Pollock is regarded as an **iconoclast** *in the art world: he challenged the conventional notion of what it meant to paint, by hurling buckets of paint at a canvas.*

From French for "destroyer of images or icons."

agnostic *(n.)* agˈnästik
One who is uncertain whether there is a higher power.

sacrilege *(n.)* sakrəlij
Violation of something considered holy.

inviolate *(adj.)* inˈvīələt
Pure, not violated or profaned.

catholic *(adj.)* kaTH(ə)lik
Universal.

ACTIVITY 37

Write the word that completes each sentence:

1. Pablo questions whether there is any higher power and so has branded himself an _____.

2. Tossing a holy book on the ground is often considered a _____ because doing so is deemed highly disrespectful.

3. After his hometown football team had gone 10 years without making the playoffs, Chad became an _____ and began following a winning team instead.

4. John Cage was a musical _____, shocking the world when he released 4'33", a piece in which no music is played for exactly 4 minutes and 33 seconds.

Religious Words (PART 2)

novitiate *(n.)* nōˈviSHēət
A person new to a religious order, or any beginner in general.

*The ski **novitiates** gingerly made their way down the bunny slope, falling every few minutes.*

From the Latin for "novice."

hagiography *(n.)* hagēˈägrəfē,
Traditionally a biography of a saint, but today any writing that praises highly to the point of worship.

*Some accounts of star athletes' performances in the sports section read like **hagiographies**.*

This word is from the root *hagio-*, which means "holy," and *-graphy*, which means "writing." The adjective *hagiographic*, which isn't nearly as mellifluous as *hagiography*, is also somewhat common.

syncretic *(adj.)* sinkrəˌtik
Describing the fusion of several different beliefs.

*Her exercise regimen is **syncretic**, incorporating Pilates, yoga, weights, high-intensity cardio training, and meditation.*

From the Greek for "uniting." The noun *syncretism* is also somewhat common.

desecrate *(v.)* desəˌkrāt
To violate something considered holy.

ecclesiastical *(adj.)* əˌklēzēˈastək(ə)l
Relating to a church or the clergy.

priggish *(adj.)* prigiSH
Sanctimonious.

anathema *(n.)* əˈnaTHəmə
An official curse against a person; someone or something intensely disliked.

ecumenical *(adj.)* ekyəˈmenək(ə)l
Aimed at uniting many different churches.

ACTIVITY 38

Mark "S" if the meanings of the two words are similar, "R" if they are related, or "NR" if they are not related:

1. anathema and ecumenical _____

2. priggish and ecclesiastical _____

3. hagiography and novitiate _____

4. desecrate and syncretic _____

Prefix *Ex-*

Ex- is a common prefix meaning "out." Here are some words, a bit on the tougher side, with the *ex-* root.

extenuate *(v.)* ikˈstenyəˌwāt
To lessen the severity.

*He tried to blame his low exam score on a variety of **extenuating** circumstances, from a bout with the flu to a lost textbook.*

This word is from the Latin for "to make small." This verb is most often used in the phrase *extenuating circumstances*, as in the sample sentence.

exonerate *(v.)* igˈzänəˌrāt
To free from blame or wrongdoing.

*The DNA evidence surfaced 20 years after the crime, and the defendant was finally **exonerated** of all wrongdoing.*

From the Latin for "to remove the burden." A less common version of this word means "to release somebody from an obligation or duty."

execrate *(v.)* eksəˌkrāt
To express strong disapproval and loathing.

*The crowd **execrated** the opposing team's star player as he stepped up to bat, hissing and booing, and even throwing empty cups on the field.*

Another word that comes from Latin, this time meaning "to curse."

expurgate *(v.)* ekspərˌgāt
To remove objectionable material from written work.

exude *(v.)* igˈzo͞od
To ooze or flow slowly.

expunge *(v.)* ikˈspənj
To wipe out any trace.

ACTIVITY 39

Complete the word for each definition:

1. to remove objectionable material from written work = ex_ur____

2. to ooze or flow slowly = ex__d_

3. to wipe out any trace = ex__ng__

4. to lessen the severity = ex___nu___

5. to free from blame = ex__er___

6. to express strong disapproval and loathing = ex__cra__

Commonly Confused Pairs (PART 1)

Tread carefully with these very similar-sounding words. Note: Since the words on this list already look alike, we decided to forgo their etymology to avoid unnecessary confusion.

flout vs. flaunt *(verbs)* flout, flônt
Flout means "to disregard in a scornful manner."

Flaunt means "to show off something in a very obvious manner."

*"Everybody rolls through stop signs," said Dmitri, once again **flouting** the rule—just as a police car pulled up behind him.*

*Terry liked to **flaunt** his biceps, always finding an excuse to wear a short-sleeved T-shirt.*

discrete vs. discreet *(adjectives)* diˈskrēt (both)
Discrete means "separated into distinct groups."

Discreet means "not drawing attention to an activity that is generally kept private."

*Though both deal with stars, astronomy and astrology are considered **discrete** realms of knowledge.*

*The new student raised his hand **discreetly** and, in a barely audible whisper, asked the teacher whether he could go to the bathroom.*

A good way to remember the difference between these two words is the *t* in discrete *separate*s the two *e*'s.

affect *(verb)* **vs. effect** *(noun)* əˈfekt (both)
Affect means "to cause something to happen."

Effect means "result, outcome."

*The amount of sleep one receives each night **affects** one's productivity the following day.*

*One **effect** of not getting enough sleep is a drop in productivity.*

venal vs. venial *(adjectives)* vēnl, vēnēəl
Venal means "open to corruption or bribery."

Venial means "forgivable or pardonable."

*The judge was revealed to be **venal**, accepting bribes from the defense for a lighter sentence.*

*Driving 10 miles over the speed limit, while clearly illegal, is **venial** compared to driving 30 miles over the speed limit.*

ACTIVITY 40

Write the word that completes each sentence:

1. Art and math are often treated as _____ realms even though the two sometimes overlap.

2. The dictatorship was _____, justice always a matter of bribing the right person.

3. Studying daily clearly has an _____ on one's GPA.

4. Once she inserted earplugs, the noise below no longer _____ her.

Commonly Confused Pairs (PART 2)

complacent vs. complaisant *(adjectives)* kəmˈplās(ə)nt, kəmˈplāsənt
Complacent means "satisfied in the moment, not thinking of the future."

Complaisant means "eager to please."

After receiving straight A's, Carter became **complacent** *and started turning his homework in late—by the next semester he had three C's.*

The normally **complaisant** *Jenny flat out refused to do any more housework.*

emigrate vs. immigrate *(verbs)* eməˌgrāt, iməˌgrāt
Emigrate means "to leave a country."

Immigrate means "to enter another country."

Her parents had initially **emigrated** *from Russia to Germany, though eventually they ended up* **immigrating** *to the United States.*

allude vs. elude *(verbs)* əˈlo͞od, ēˈlo͞od
Allude means "to reference something by not mentioning it specifically."

Elude means "to evade capture."

Fred **alluded** *to the movie he was planning to watch this weekend, quoting: "In a galaxy far, far away."*

For three long weeks, the bank thieves **eluded** *the authorities, until a helicopter spotted their hideout.*

censor vs. censure *(verbs)* sensər, sen(t)SHər
Censor means "to remove the objectionable parts from something."

Censure means "to criticize someone harshly."

During the 1980s, profanity was **censored** *on TV using a loud beep, so lip-readers were often left mortified.*

An independent committee **censured** *the CEO for embezzling funds.*

ACTIVITY 41

Write the word that completes each sentence:

1. The new nanny was _____, eager to make sure the children were happy.

2. He had squandered his father's wealth, and for that he was _____.

3. Given the ominous change in government, the family considered _____ to Europe.

4. Throughout history, people have attempted to _____ Shakespeare's work by removing the text referring to certain parts of the human anatomy.

5. Up by 10 runs in the last inning of the game, the team became _____ and nearly ended up losing.

6. He struggled at trivia games because even when he knew the answer, it would often _____ him.

Commonly Confused Pairs (PART 3)

elicit *(verb)* **vs. illicit** *(adjective)* ēˈlisət, i(l)ˈlisit
Elicit means "to draw out, usually a reaction."

Illicit means "illegal."

*His puns, as terrible as they are, never fail to **elicit** a laugh from his friends.*

*The **illicit** drug trade has intensified in recent years.*

flounder vs. founder *(verbs)* floundər, foundər
Flounder means "to flail about, either literally or figuratively."

Founder means "to sink, either literally or figuratively."

*The three young ducklings **floundered** in the mud as they tried to keep pace with their mother.*

*The space team miscalculated the amount of energy needed to reach Mars, so the project **foundered**.*

prescribe vs. proscribe *(verbs)* prəˈskrīb, prōˈskrīb
Prescribe means "to recommend, as a course of treatment."

Proscribe means "to ban."

*The doctor **prescribed** rest and lots of ice for the patient with the broken arm.*

*The books of James Joyce are **proscribed** in certain countries for their many references to bodily excretions.*

torturous vs. tortuous *(adjectives)* tôrCH(ə)rəs, tôrCH(o͞o)əs
Torturous means "extremely painful."

Tortuous means "full of twists, winding."

*Everyone finds at least one genre of music so **torturous** that they'd rather plug their ears than listen to a single second of it.*

*Though the distance from the base to the summit was only a mile, the ascent was so **tortuous** that the hikers took nearly nine hours to reach the top.*

ACTIVITY 42

Write the word that completes each sentence:

1. The start-up _____ soon after its inception because it never figured out how to make money.

2. Were this sentence to carry on for an entire paragraph, full of twist and turns, unnecessary phrases, and the like, it would be _____.

3. To minimize the number of on-field injuries, professional football has _____ late tackles.

4. She had become so implacable over time that there was no way to _____ even a modicum of sympathy.

5. For someone with a bad back, a 12-hour road trip would be _____.

Annoying Words

The lesson title says it all!

irksome *(adj.)* ərksəm
Annoying.

His new roommate quickly became **irksome** *as he told one bad joke after another.*

This comes from German, meaning "to annoy." Good synonyms to know are *galling* and *exasperating*.

ingratiate *(v.)* inˈgrāSHēˌāt
To try to win another's favor, often through flattery.

Ricky tried to **ingratiate** *himself with the other boys in his school, but many quickly grew tired of him complimenting them on their attire.*

From Latin and Italian, meaning "to seek favor." Someone who is ingratiating can often be annoying.

cloying *(adj.)* kloiNG
Overly sentimental to the point of being disgusting.

The newlywed couple repelled many of their friends by calling each other **cloying** *names like "honey-bunny" and "snuggle-bug."*

This word comes from the Middle English for "being in excess to the point of loathing." This word should be reserved for cases in which the sentimentality is so over the top as to be sickening.

aggravate *(v.)* agrəˌvāt
To make worse.

vex *(v.)* veks
To annoy.

gall *(v.)* gôl
To annoy.

mawkish *(adj.)* môkiSH
Overly sentimental and cloying.

ACTIVITY 43

Mark "S" if the meanings of the two words are similar, "R" if they are related, or "NR" if they are not related:

1. mawkish and cloying _____

2. gall and vex _____

3. ingratiate and aggravate _____

What Did You Call Me?

There are many words that mean "to slander or say nasty things about a person." For some reason, these seem to outnumber the words that mean "to praise."

libel *(n.)* lībəl
Slander in writing.

*The celebrity tweeted false, hurtful things about her rival, and a month later was sued for **libel**.*

From Latin, describing a small legal book. *Libel* is typically used when referring to defamation in writing; *slander* is defamation in speech.

besmirch *(v.)* besmirCH
To dirty or hurt another's reputation.

*Just by being seen in public with the gang of criminals, Marty knew his reputation had been **besmirched**.*

A *smirch* is a dirty mark. *Tarnish*, *blacken*, and *sully* are three synonyms for *besmirch*.

raillery *(n.)* rālərē
Teasing.

*To his friends, their jeers were nothing more than **raillery**; to him they stung deeply.*

From the French for "to tease." Unlike all these other hurtful words, *raillery* refers to good-natured teasing.

scurrilous *(adj.)* skərələs
Using or given to coarse language.

calumny *(n.)* kaləmnē
Slander.

vilify *(v.)* vilə͵fī
To say evil things about someone.

impugn *(v.)* im'pyo̅o̅n
To cast doubt on another's character and integrity.

traduce *(v.)* trə'd(y)o̅o̅s
To slander and cause disgrace.

ACTIVITY 44

Provide the word for the given definition:

1. teasing = _____

2. to dirty or hurt another's reputation = _____

3. to cast doubt on another's character and integrity = _____

4. defame, slander = (2 synonyms) _____

Courtroom Words

Courtroom lingo has given us many words that often apply to a broader context.

verdict *(n.)* vərdikt
A judgment, usually offered in a courtroom.

*After much deliberation, the **verdict** announced by the panel was that the director was looking for a quick buck and had compromised his standards when making the sequel to his previous blockbuster.*

From the Latin for "truth" and "to say." This word can also describe a general opinion.

tort *(n.)* tôrt
A wrongful act other than a breach of contract.

*The law professor focused on **tort** law, discussing with her students the many cases in which an individual had suffered injuries due to another's negligence.*

This word comes from Middle English for "injury."

litigious *(adj.)* ləˈtijəs
Inclined to sue others.

*The automobile company was highly **litigious**, claiming that other companies had copied its award-winning designs.*

From the Old French for "lawsuit." This word doesn't necessarily have to relate to speech but to any purported crime that ends up being tried in a court of law.

acquit *(v.)* əˈkwit
To declare not guilty in a trial.

subpoena *(n.)* səˈpēnə
A document summoning one to court.

affidavit *(n.)* afəˈdāvit
A written statement presented in court that is offered up under oath.

exculpate *(v.)* ekskəlˌpāt
To free from blame.

ACTIVITY 45

Match the word with its definition:

1. to declare not guilty in a trial _____

2. to free from blame _____

3. a document summoning one to court _____

4. inclined to sue others _____

5. a judgment, usually offered in a courtroom _____

a. verdict

b. subpoena

c. acquit

d. exculpate

e. litigious

Give Peace a Chance

Ranging from peaceful to combative, the following words are important to know, whether you are an avid reader or are preparing for a standardized test.

appease *(v.)* əˈpēz
To make less angry.

The small country attempted to **appease** *the dictator of the neighboring country by removing tariffs on its luxury goods.*

Originally from the Latin for "peace." *Placate* and *pacify* are two synonyms that are very common.

implacable *(adj.)* imˈplakəb(ə)l
Unable to make less angry.

When Max's mother saw that he had broken her prized vase, she became **implacable** *and Max, fearing the repercussions, bolted out the front door.*

From the Latin for the word for "appease" and *im-* for the opposite.

contentious *(adj.)* kənˈten(t)SHəs
Inclined to argue.

Even if he knew little about the topic, he was so **contentious** *that he had to find something about it he didn't agree with.*

The word is derived from *contend*, as in "to argue a point." This can be a misleading word because its first seven letters—*content*—imply happiness.

pugnacious *(adj.)*
pəgˈnāSHəs
Inclined to fight, combative.

conciliatory *(adj.)*
kənˈsilēəˌtôrē
Inclined to making peace.

truculent *(adj.)* trəkyələnt
Ready to pick a fight.

jingoist *(n.)* jiNGgōˌist
Patriotic and constantly calling for war.

propitiate *(v.)*
prəˈpiSHēˌāt
To appease or placate.

ACTIVITY 46

Complete the word for each definition:

1. A synonym for appease = pro_____

2. A synonym for pugnacious = con_____

3. One who wants their country to wage war = _____ist

4. Unable to be calmed or pacified = imp_____

5. Ready to pick a fight = _____cul___

6. Wanting to make peace = _____atory

Frightening Words

These words describe a range of fears, from mildly anxious to full of terror.

apprehension *(n.)* aprəˈhenSHən
Fear or anxiety about the future.

With college graduation near and no job prospects in sight, his **apprehension** *was on the rise.*

From the Latin for "to grasp." Another definition of *apprehension*—the seizing of a criminal—is commonly used.

petrified *(adj.)* petrəˌfīd
So frightened as to be unable to move.

The hikers were **petrified** *the moment they saw the mountain lion pounce from behind a bush.*

Comes from the Latin for "rock."

macabre *(adj.)* məˈkäbrə
Gruesome, involving blood and death.

The **macabre** *crime scene was surrounded by yellow tape.*

This is from the French *danse macabre*, or "dance of death."

grisly *(adj.)* ˈgrizlē
Gory, gruesome.

morbid *(adj.)* môrbəd
Grisly.

phantasmagorical *(adj.)*
fanˌtazməˈgôrikəl
Characterized by many suddenly changing images, as in a nightmare or hallucination.

horripilation *(n.)*
hôˌripəˈlāSHən
Goose bumps.

ACTIVITY 47

Mark "S" if the meanings of the two words are similar, "R" if they are related, or "NR" if they are not related:

1. morbid and grisly _____

2. macabre and phantasmagorical _____

3. petrified and apprehensive _____

Group Dynamics

Many words relate to groups—whether you are in them, out of them, or hoping to be a part of one.

ostracize *(v.)* ästrə‚sīz
To actively shun or exclude someone from a group.

*Once his friends found out that Max had been spreading false rumors about them, they swiftly **ostracized** him.*

In ancient Greece, the names of unpopular people were written on broken shards of pottery known as *ostrakon*, hence the word "ostracize."

hierarchy *(n.)* hī(ə)‚rärkē
The existence of levels of power or status separating individuals.

*The company preached a flat **hierarchy** in which everyone could voice an opinion; in reality, the decisions were typically made by those at the top.*

From the Greek for "sacred ruler." This word was first used to describe a ranking of angels.

schism *(n.)* s(k)izəm
A major rift within a large group.

*After losing three consecutive elections, the political party underwent a major **schism**, with some members no longer speaking to others.*

From the Old French for a "split" or "cleft" (think chin). Historically this word referred to the Great Schism of 1054 and other ecclesiastical rifts, but today it can be applied to any group.

banish *(v.)* baniSH
To remove or drive out from a home or community.

clique *(n.)* klēk
A group that is exclusionary.

coterie *(n.)* kōdərē,
A group that has shared interests.

interdependence *(n.)* in(t)ərdə'pendəns
The reliance of those in a group on one another.

synergy *(n.)* sinərjē
The quality of a group working together, in which the product is greater than the sum of the individuals.

ACTIVITY 48

Write the word that completes each sentence:

1. The individual members of the group were not among the top in the organization, yet their _____ was so remarkable that they won first place.

2. The group had long experienced serious internal conflict, so the _____ surprised few.

3. Tae Kwon Do has a built-in _____ based on the color of one's belt, all the way from novice (white belt) to master (black belt).

Mark "S" if the meanings of the two words are similar, "R" if they are related, or "NR" if they are not related:

4. interdependence and synergy _____

5. clique and coterie _____

6. banish and ostracize _____

Governmental Words

Many words in English describe governments and, perhaps not surprisingly, many are negative.

beneficent *(adj.)* bəˈnefəsənt
Promoting good.

*The queen was **beneficent**, always redistributing wealth to ensure a higher quality of living among her people.*

From the Latin *ben-* "for good." The noun form of the word is *beneficence*.

oppressive *(adj.)* əˈpresiv
Overpowering, tyrannical.

*After years of relative beneficence, the government became **oppressive** the moment citizens began to demand more freedoms.*

Comes from the Latin for "pressed against." This word can also describe weather (e.g., oppressive heat and humidity) or moods (e.g., a feeling of oppressive apprehension).

despot *(n.)* despət
A ruler who treats people harshly.

*The twentieth century will be remembered in part for its **despots**— those who rule with complete power, murdering scores of civilians at a whim.*

From the Greek for "absolute ruler." *Tyrant*, *dictator*, and *autocrat* are related words, and can have the same connotation of cruelty.

autocratic *(adj.)*
ôdəˈkradik
Ruling with sole power.

subjugate *(v.)* səbjəˌgāt
To make submissive.

tyrant *(n.)* tīrənt
A ruler who governs with complete power and often cruelly.

ACTIVITY 49

Unscramble the word and define:

1. rantyt _____

2. posted _____

3. coatauctir _____

4. justbegua _____

Words of Scale

We earlier examined words describing amount. Now we look at words expressing size, from the tiniest to the most enormous.

behemoth *(n.)* bəˈhēməTH
Anything extremely large.

*The one-time small company had grown into a **behemoth**, competing (and often dominating) in more than a dozen markets.*

This comes from the Hebrew for "beast." This word shows up in the Old Testament and while some believe it refers to a mythological beast, others believe that it might actually refer to an elephant, or even a hippopotamus.

diminutive *(adj.)* dəˈminyədiv
Very tiny.

*Though she cut a **diminutive** figure, not an inch over five feet tall, the governor mustered the authority of a hundred generals.*

From the Latin for "diminished." This word can also describe words that have a suffix added to them suggesting smallness, as in the -*let* in *booklet*.

prodigious *(adj.)* prəˈdijəs
Great in degree or extent.

*Catherine's memory was **prodigious**: She could recite dozens of epic poems by heart.*

The Latin and French predecessors of this word meant "ominous," a slightly negative connotation. *Immense* and *vast* are two related words.

immense *(adj.)* iˈmens
Large and vast.

gargantuan *(adj.)*
gärˈgan(t)SH(oō)ən
Tremendous in size, volume, or degree.

colossal *(adj.)* kəˈläsəl
Bulk of an astonishing degree.

Lilliputian *(adj.)*
liləˈpyoōSH(ə)n
Extremely small.

ACTIVITY 50

Mark "S" if the meanings of the two words are similar, "O" if they are opposite, or "D" if they are different:

1. immense and prodigious _____

2. behemoth and Lilliputian _____

3. colossal and gargantuan _____

How's It Going?

Life can throw you lemons or lemonade. Below are words that describe the various ups and downs of life.

travail *(n.)* ˈtraˌvāl
Pain and difficulty related to work.

*Sandy did not anticipate the **travail** that came from being in the constant limelight, wishing that fans would leave her alone.*

This word comes from Latin for "a torture device involving three stakes." The word *travel*, which for many conjures up sandy beaches and hammocks, is derived from *travail*; at one time, travel involved laborious journeys by carriages along dangerous routes.

arduous *(adj.)* ˈärjo͞oəs
Involving intense effort and difficulty.

*Though the map showed the top of the peak as only a mile away, it did not indicate just how **arduous** the ascent would be.*

From the Latin for "steep." *Arduous* can be used in any context, not just mountains.

halcyon *(adj.)* halsēən
Calm, happy.

*For many, the 1920s were **halcyon** days, at least compared to the travails brought on by the Great Depression.*

This word comes from Greek mythology and describes a large bird that, by merely flapping its wings, calmed the ocean waters. *Halcyon* is often coupled with *days*; it originally described the 14 days of winter when the waters off Greece were the calmest.

tumultuous *(adj.)*
t(y)o͞oˈməlCHo͞oəs
Chaotic and disorderly.

turbulent *(adj.)*
tərbyələnt
Marked by disorder.

tribulation *(n.)*
tribyəˈlāSH(ə)n
Difficulty, hardship.

vicissitude *(n.)*
vəˈsisəˌt(y)o͞od
The inevitable ups and downs of life.

ACTIVITY 51

Mark "S" if the meanings of the two words are similar, "R" if they are related, or "NR" if they are not related:

1. turbulent and tumultuous _____

2. arduous and halcyon _____

3. travail and vicissitude _____

Write the word that completes each sentence:

4. She had experienced triumphs and defeats, she had seen halcyon days and turbulent days, in a decade of _____.

5. One bad thing after another befell Peter, and he lamented this constant barrage of _____.

Attention to Detail

Do you inspect every nook and cranny, or do you just go with the flow?

quibble *(v.)* kwibəl
To raise trivial objections.

*Though Bobby was able to hit home runs with ease, the coach continued to **quibble** over his stance.*

Comes from the Latin for "petty objection." This word can also be a noun, meaning "a small objection, usually over something trivial."

cursory *(adj.)* kərs(ə)rē
Not thorough.

*Even a **cursory** examination by the border patrol revealed that the man was carrying banned produce.*

From the Latin for "runner." A good way to remember this word is to think of a cursor, which is the blinking (often vertical) line when you are typing on the computer. It doesn't stay solid for a long time before it blinks again. Likewise, something that is cursory doesn't stick around for a long time.

fastidious *(adj.)* faˈstidēəs
Extremely attentive to detail, to the point of being nitpicky.

*He was **fastidious** about his hair, habitually spending an hour each day fussing with the part.*

This word comes from the Latin for "loathing." It can also be traced back to *disagreeable* and *disgusted*.

scrutinize *(v.)* skro̅o̅tn͟ˌīz
To examine very carefully.

slipshod *(adj.)* slipˌSHäd
Careless, typically in the way something is put together.

meticulous *(adj.)* məˈtikyələs
Attentive to detail, but without the negative connotation of *fastidious*.

persnickety *(adj.)* pərˈsnikədē
Nitpicky, fastidious.

perfunctory *(adj.)* pərˈfəNG(k)t(ə)rē
Not paying attention to detail, going through the motions.

ACTIVITY 52

Write the word that completes the sentence:

1. Martin gained a reputation for being _____, always finding something to _____ about if everything wasn't 100 percent tidy. (2 possible answers)

2. Many do homework in a way that is _____, completing the assignment but putting little heart into it.

3. The building codes were lax, so the building was constructed in a _____ manner.

4. Ever the fastidious editor, Carol would _____ text, knowing that inevitably an error would jump off the page.

5. The teacher was always pressed for time and could rarely give little more than a _____ examination of each student's assignment.

The Facts of Life

The following words cover birth to death—and everything in between.

juvenile (n.) jo͞ovəˌnīl
A young person.

He was still a juvenile and therefore couldn't sign the court papers.

From the Latin for "young person." The word can also be used as an adjective, as in the phrase *juvenile delinquent*, which refers to a young person who commits a minor crime.

senile (adj.) sēˌnīl
Having deteriorating abilities as a result of old age.

Even at the age of 90, Mr. Perkins was far from senile, his razor wit undiminished.

From the Latin for "old man." The *sen-* shows up in the word *senior*, which can be used to describe somebody who is old (as in senior citizen) or can be a noun for an old person.

embryonic (adj.) embrēˈänik
In the earliest stages, not yet fully formed.

His travel plans are at best embryonic: All he knows is that he's taking three weeks to travel somewhere in Asia.

Comes from the Latin for "embryo." *Rudimentary* and the less common *inchoate* are synonyms.

geriatric (adj.) jerēˈatrik
Relating to old age.

fledgling (adj.) flejliNG
Young, novice, inexperienced.

callow (adj.) kalō
Immature, usually referring to a young, inexperienced person.

moribund (adj.)
môrəˌbənd
Near death, dormant.

chrysalis (n.) krisələs
A protective stage of development.

ACTIVITY 53

Write the word that completes each sentence:

1. Given that symphony halls across the country are shutting down, many argue that classical music is becoming _____.

2. Business school was a _____ for Rick, where he learned the skills that would help him become a successful CEO years later.

3. The dog had become _____ and struggled to find its way home.

Provide the word for the given definition:

4. young, inexperienced (2 possible answers) = _____

5. relating to old age = _____

6. a young person = _____

It's Debatable

The art of argumentation is more than just a series of heated exchanges. Below are words that capture the breadth and subtlety of debate.

concede *(v.)* kənˈsēd
To admit that another person's argument or point of view has some validity.

*Though Sarah didn't agree at all with Bill's political stance, she had to **concede** that on a few points he was right.*

Comes from the Latin *com-*, meaning "with" and *cedere*, meaning "yield." The noun form of the word is *concession* (though do not confuse this with a concession, which is a food and refreshment stand at some larger venues).

maintain *(v.)* mānˈtān
To state strongly.

*The authors of the study **maintain** that the brain continues to grow well into adulthood.*

From Latin for "to hold in the hand." *Maintain* also means "to sustain" or "to keep something functioning."

parry *(v.)* parē
To block or ward off an attack.

*Despite the many counter-objections her opponent made, Flora **parried** each with pizzazz.*

This word is from the French for "to ward off" and is a term used in fencing, when the opponent's foil (saber) is blocked. When used in a verbal context, *parry* is similar to the words *evade* and *sidestep*.

forensics *(n.)* fəˈrenzik
Scientific tests or techniques used in connection with the detection of crime.

riposte *(n.)* riˈpōst
A quick (usually witty) verbal reply.

unassailable *(adj.)* ənəˈsāləb(ə)l
Immune to attack.

ACTIVITY 54

Provide the word for the given definition:

1. immune to attack = _____

2. a quick (usually witty) verbal reply = _____

3. scientific tests or techniques used in connection with the detection of crime = _____

4. to block or ward off an attack = _____

5. to state strongly = _____

It's a Party!

A party can make one person get a little out of control while another hides in the corner. The following words describe some of the points along that broad spectrum.

affable *(adj.)* afəb(ə)l
Friendly and outgoing.

*In public, Greg was **affable** and always eager to meet people.*

From Old French for "to speak." Two good synonyms to know are *amiable* and *congenial*.

inebriated *(adj.)* iˈnēbrēˌātəd
Drunk.

*The high school reunion was full of old, **inebriated** men.*

This comes from the Latin for "to intoxicate." This word is typically used casually, whereas *intoxicated* is used in a clinical context.

retiring *(adj.)* rəˈtī(ə)riNG
Timid and preferring to be alone.

*Whenever the lights dimmed and the music started thumping, Dexter became **retiring**, finding a corner and not moving for the duration of the party.*

Comes from the French for "to withdraw," as in finding a safe place. In the context of a party, a retiring person could be called a *wallflower*.

extrovert *(n.)* ekstrəˌvərt
A person who is naturally outgoing.

introvert *(n.)* intrəˌvərt
A person who prefers to keep to him- or herself.

debauchery *(n.)*
dəˈbôCHərē
Extreme indulgence in pleasurable activities.

expansive *(adj.)*
ikˈspansiv
Outgoing and sociable.

ACTIVITY 55

Provide the word for the given definition:

1. a person who is naturally outgoing = _____

2. extreme indulgence in pleasurable activities = _____

3. drunk = _____

4. timid and preferring to be alone (besides *introverted*) = _____

5. friendly and outgoing = _____

Describing the Landscape

From landscapes teeming with plants to an old, red barn, these words capture a variety of different landscapes.

verdant *(adj.)* vərdnt
Green, usually because of lush vegetation.

*The March rains left the hills a **verdant** green.*

From the Latin for "green."

rustic *(adj.)* rəstik
Describing the charming aspects of the countryside.

*The property was **rustic**: A small red barn sat next to a verdant hillside, where cows grazed idly.*

This is from the Latin for "countryside." *Rustic* can also be a noun for a person living in a rural area, though it is used pejoratively.

bucolic *(adj.)* byo͞oˈkälik
Describing the pleasant aspects of the country.

*Irene hopes to retire to a **bucolic** farm, where she can grow her own vegetables.*

From the Greek for "herdsmen." *Bucolic* is a synonym of *rustic*.

inhospitable *(adj.)*
inhäˈspidəb(ə)l
Describing a climate that is harsh and unfriendly to life.

lush *(adj.)* ləSH
Luxuriant, abundant.

barren *(adj.)* berən
Describing soil or fields in which nothing can grow.

pastoral *(adj.)* pastərəl
Describing the charming aspects of the country.

idyllic *(adj.)* īˈdilik
Describing a happy place or time.

ACTIVITY 56

Write the word for each definition:

1. describing the pleasant, charming aspect of the countryside (3 answers) = _____

2. green, usually because of lush vegetation = _____

3. characterized by abundance = _____

4. describing soil or fields in which nothing can grow = _____

5. describing a happy place or time = _____

It's About Time (PART 1)

The following words relate to some aspect of time, whether the shortest of intervals or the never-ending.

chronic *(adj.)* kränik
Describing a problem or disease that is long-lasting.

Chronic budgetary issues have resulted in roads riddled with potholes.

From the Greek root *chromos-* meaning "time." This word can also describe a negative personality trait, e.g., chronically late, and is also often used to describe ongoing medical conditions.

perennial *(adj.)* pəˈrenēəl
Lasting for a long time or recurring over a long period.

*The **perennial** winners in professional sports tend to attract fans from all over the country.*

Comes from the Latin for "lasting through the year." Unlike *chronic*, *perennial* does not have a negative connotation.

ephemeral *(adj.)* əˈfem(ə)rəl
Not lasting a long time, short lived.

*Hit songs have an **ephemeral** life, hardly played on the radio a year after their initial release.*

Originally a Medieval Latin medical term meaning "a fever that lasted a day." Poets sometimes use the mayfly, which lives for only a few hours, to symbolize the ephemeral aspects of life.

transient *(adj.)* tranzēənt
Not lasting a long time.

perpetual *(adj.)*
pərˈpeCH(o͞o)əl
Going on and on, without end, seemingly forever.

interminable *(adj.)*
inˈtərmənəb(ə)l
Without end.

immemorial *(adj.)*
i(m)məˈmôrēəl
Originating a very long time ago.

evanescent *(adj.)*
evəˈnes(ə)nt
Fleeting, of short duration.

ACTIVITY 57

Mark "S" if the meanings of the two words are similar, "O" if they are opposite, or "D" if they are different:

1. immemorial and perpetual _____

2. evanescent and transient _____

3. chronic and perennial _____

4. ephemeral and interminable _____

It's About Time (PART 2)

intermittent *(adj.)* in(t)ərˈmitnt
Occurring on and off, but not at regular intervals.

*The rain was **intermittent**, falling in bursts one minute and then easing up for a few minutes and even stopping altogether.*

From the Latin for "letting go between." The word *sporadic* is a good synonym to know.

incessant *(adj.)* inˈses(ə)nt
Describing something negative that is constant.

*Much to the teacher's dismay, the two students chatted **incessantly** during class, even when he had moved them to opposite sides of the classroom.*

This comes from the Latin for "not ceasing." *Persistent* is a more common word that means more or less the same thing.

sporadic *(adj.)* spəˈradik
Occurring at random intervals.

*Well past midnight, **sporadic** explosions from fireworks jolted many awake just as sleep was approaching.*

From the Greek for "scattered." *Scattered* and *irregular* are good synonyms.

erratic *(adj.)* əˈradik
Highly irregular and unpredictable.

fitful *(adj.)* fitfəl
Occurring intermittently.

desultory *(adj.)* desəlˌtôrē
Lacking a plan, unfocused.

horology *(n.)* həˈräləjē
The study of time and clock making.

ACTIVITY 58

Mark "S" if the meanings of the two words are similar, "O" if they are opposite, or "D" if they are different:

1. desultory and incessant _____

2. horology and erratic _____

3. fitful and erratic _____

4. sporadic and intermittent _____

The Times They Are A-Changing

Revolutions and riots have long led to a change in leadership. Here are a few words that capture this phenomenon.

turmoil *(n.)* tər͵moil
A state of great confusion and unrest.

The prime minister's sudden resignation threw the country into **turmoil.**

The origin of this word is uncertain. Common synonyms include *disturbance* and *agitation.*

upheaval *(n.)* əpˈhēvəl
A sudden, massive change.

The economic **upheaval** *of late 2008 led to the collapse of several large financial institutions.*

This word comes from Frisian, a language closely related to English and German. This word is also used in geology when referring to a sudden upward shift in the Earth's crust.

junta *(n.)* ho͞on(t)ə
A military group that seizes power by violent means.

Dictatorships are often the result of **juntas** *in which a military general takes control and does not want to give up power.*

Comes from the Latin for "to join." This word also describes a sixteenth-century legislative council in Portugal and Spain.

concord *(n.)* käNG͵kôrd
Agreement, harmony.

cataclysmic *(adj.)*
kadəˈklizəmik
Catastrophic.

usurp *(v.)* yo͞oˈsərp
To seize power, usually by violent means.

stasis *(n.)* stāsis
A state of inactivity.

ACTIVITY 59

Write the word that completes each sentence:

1. The _____ was able to _____ power during a midnight raid on the palace.

2. The meteor that struck the Earth nearly 65 million years ago was _____, leading to the extinction of the dinosaurs.

3. After the company's president was arrested for income-tax evasion, days of _____ followed, with the company's future uncertain.

4. The two clans that had been at war for decades signed a treaty establishing _____.

Secondary Meanings (PART 1)

The following words have secondary meanings that are not particularly common and might even surprise you. Rather than give you the word history of the original term, which wouldn't help you remember the secondary definitions here, I've omitted the word history altogether.

flag *(v.)* flag
To lose energy, tire.

*Around the two-hour mark, the audience's attention began to **flag**, and by the third hour, half of them had walked out of the film.*

From Old English for "hanging loosely" or "drooping." Another definition, and one that is also a verb, is "to mark something" (usually an item on a list) that requires attention.

beam *(v.)* bēm
To smile fully, from cheek to cheek.

*When she heard she was getting a major salary increase, she couldn't help but **beam**.*

Derived from Old English and meaning "ray of light." Another definition, and one that is also a verb, is "to transmit a radio signal."

hamper *(v.)* hampər
To hold back or restrain.

*She still was able to lead her team to victory despite being **hampered** by a bad cold.*

This comes from the German for "restrain." *Hinder* is a good synonym.

minute *(adj.)*
mī'n(y)ōot
Tiny, small.

graze *(v.)* grāz
To touch slightly or scrape.

refuse *(n.)* ref͵yōos
Garbage.

appropriate *(v.)*
ə'prōprē͵āt
To take by force.

graft *(n.)* graft
Corruption.

ACTIVITY 60

Match the word with its definition:

1. graze _____
2. minute _____
3. hamper _____
4. appropriate _____
5. beam _____
6. graft _____
7. flag _____
8. refuse _____

a. corruption
b. to smile fully, from cheek to cheek
c. to lose energy, tire
d. to hold back or restrain
e. garbage
f. tiny, small
g. to touch lightly or scrape
h. to take by force

Secondary Meanings (PART 2)

harbor *(v.)* härbər
To contain, conceal, give shelter.

Jeffry had long harbored resentment toward his older brother, hiding it behind false smiles.

Though the thesaurus lists words like *nurture* and *foster*, *harbor* is notably different because it can also refer to something negative.

tender *(v.)* tendər
To offer up, usually something formal.

He was so put off by the company's culture that he tendered his resignation after only three weeks.

Money is considered *legal tender*, meaning it can be offered up as a way of paying for something.

score *(n.)* skôr
A large number.

When the author revealed that she would release the final book in her trilogy, scores of people lined up outside the nation's bookstores.

Two other common words—*raft* and *host*—also have a secondary meaning of "a large number."

weather *(v.)* weTHər
To withstand something difficult.

wax *(v.)* waks
To increase in size.

temper *(v.)* tempər
To soften the effect of something.

table *(v.)* tābəl
To put aside for future consideration.

patent *(adj.)* patnt
Glaringly obvious.

ACTIVITY 61

Match the word with its definition:

1. wax _____
2. table _____
3. temper _____
4. weather _____
5. score _____
6. harbor _____
7. tender _____
8. patent _____

a. glaringly obvious

b. to offer up formally

c. to soften the effect of something

d. to contain, conceal, give shelter

e. to put aside for future consideration

f. to increase in size

g. a large number

h. to withstand something difficult

Secondary Meanings (PART 3)

refrain *(v.)* rəˈfrān
To hold oneself back from doing something.

*Though Timmy couldn't wait to eat his pizza, he **refrained** from doing so until the rest of his family was seated.*

This comes from the Latin *frenum-*, which is a bridle, or something that restrains. The noun form refers to the chorus of a song, specifically the repeated lines.

fleece *(v.)* flēs
To cheat or swindle.

*It was only when Harry arrived at the theater did he realized he'd been **fleeced**: The tickets were fake and he was denied entry.*

From the Old English word for the wool coat of a sheep. The term *fleece* also refers to the coat of a sheep.

grouse *(v.)* grous
To complain or grumble.

*The people at the bus stop **groused** in unison when a second packed bus passed them without stopping.*

This word is of uncertain origin, although it resembles a Normandy French dialect word for "grumble" or "complain." A *grouse* is a large game bird.

telling *(adj.)* teliNG
Revealing.

list *(v.)* list
To tilt to one side.

becoming *(adj.)*
bəˈkəmiNG
Suitable, apt.

intimate *(v.)* in(t)əˌmāt
To suggest subtly.

entrance *(v.)* entrəns
To hold spellbound.

ACTIVITY 62

Match the word with its definition:

1. entrance _____
2. becoming _____
3. refrain _____
4. intimate _____
5. grouse _____
6. fleece _____
7. list _____
8. telling _____

a. revealing
b. to hold oneself back from doing something
c. to cheat or swindle
d. to complain or grumble
e. to tilt to one side
f. suitable, apt
g. to hold spellbound
h. to suggest subtly

Secondary Meanings (PART 4)

start *(n.)* start
A sudden movement.

*The sound of dishes crashing upstairs gave everyone a **start**.*

This word comes from the Old English for "jumping around." This word can also be used as a verb. You have to rely on context to determine which *start* is being referred to.

check *(v.)* CHek
To restrain, hold back.

*Unless the growth of weeds is **checked**, they are going to engulf the entire property.*

This meaning of *check* comes from an Old French word and harks back to the game of chess. It is still used in the game to this day. *Check*, as it is used here, can also be a noun, as in *to keep in check*.

flush *(v.)* fləSH
To force something out into the open.

*The authorities **flushed** the criminals out of hiding by releasing attack dogs.*

From the Latin *fluxus*, which means "flow." This word is traditionally used to refer to driving animals out of hiding.

involved *(adj.)* inˈvälvd
Intricate and complicated.

qualify *(v.)* kwäləˌfī
To limit or restrict a statement.

fell *(adj.)* fel
Evil.

arch *(adj.)* ärCH
Playfully teasing.

ACTIVITY 63

Match the word with its definition:

1. intricate and complicated _____

2. to limit or restrict a statement _____

3. evil _____

4. to restrain, hold back _____

5. playfully teasing _____

6. a sudden movement _____

a. fell

b. arch

c. to qualify

d. start

e. to check

f. involved

How Are You Feeling?

exhilarated *(adj.)* igˈziləˌrātəd
Extremely excited and happy.

*She was **exhilarated** when she found out she'd picked all six winning lotto numbers.*

This comes from the Latin for "make cheerful." This word is similar to *thrilled*.

blithe *(adj.)* blīTH
Carefree and happy.

*Caught up in their conversation, the two friends displayed **blithe** disregard to the fact that their midterm had already begun.*

This word comes from German for "joyous." Somebody who is *blithe* is happy but at the expense of worrying about legitimate concerns. As such, this word can sometimes carry a slightly negative connotation.

ambivalent *(adj.)* amˈbivələnt
Feeling both positive and negative feelings toward something.

*He was **ambivalent** on the first day of school: He was finally able to see his friends, but he would have homework every night.*

From the Latin, *ambi-* meaning "both" and *valent* meaning "side." This word has long been a favorite of the SAT verbal section.

elated *(adj.)* iˈlātəd
Extremely happy.

melancholic *(adj.)*
melənˈkälik
Sad but in a way that one indulges in that sadness.

dour *(adj.)* do͞or
Persistently glum and pessimistic.

morose *(adj.)* məˈrōs
Sullen, gloomy.

saturnine *(adj.)* satərˌnīn
Gloomy, surly.

ACTIVITY 64

Complete the word for the given definition:

1. having mixed feelings = am_____ent

2. depressed or gloomy = sa_____ne, mo___se

3. constantly down = _ o _ r

4. very happy = e_____ed

5. carefree and happy = b____he

Time Periods

Time periods can be broken down into many different lengths. Here are a few you should know.

fortnight *(n.)* fôrt͵nīt
A period lasting two weeks.

Training for her first marathon, Sarah raced every day for a fortnight, increasing her distance each time.

From Old English for "fourteen nights." *Fortnight* has become old-fashioned and is not nearly as common these days as *two weeks*, when describing a fourteen-day period.

bimonthly *(adv.)* bīˈmənθlē
Occurring once every two months.

The magazine is published bimonthly, too infrequently for many of its fans.

Bi- means two. A good way to distinguish this from *semimonthly* is to remember that *bi-* means "two" and *semi-* means "half" or "partly."

semimonthly *(adv.)* semēˈmənθlē
Occurring twice a month.

The network used to have semimonthly broadcasts of bowling tournaments, until ratings became so low that they canceled the broadcast altogether.

Semi- means "half."

antediluvian *(adj.)*
antēdəˈlo͞ovēən
Extremely old or ancient (literally "before the flood").

fin-de-siècle *(adj.)*
fan də sēˈəkl(ə)
Describing the period at the end of the nineteenth century.

crepuscular *(adj.)*
krəˈpəskyələr
Describing the evening.

ACTIVITY 65

Complete the word for the given definition:

1. describing the evening = cre_____ar

2. extremely old or ancient = ant____ian

3. describing the time period before the nineteenth century = f__-de-s__e

4. occurring twice a month = _____mont___

5. happening once every two months = _____mont___

6. a period lasting two weeks = fo____ht

Flavor

Words that relate to flavor, from bland to delectable, often apply in more general contexts as well.

insipid *(adj.)* inˈsipid
Lacking flavor, dull and uninteresting.

The critic found the movie **insipid***; the characters were two-dimensional and the plot predictable.*

From the French for "not tasteful." *Insipid* can refer to beverages (e.g., the insipid coffee at rest stops) or a creative product (e.g., another insipid Top 40 hit).

vapid *(adj.)* vapid
Lacking originality or stimulating ideas.

Many find the 1980s **vapid** *as far as entertainment goes; bloody action flicks, synthesizer rock, and laugh-track sitcoms predominated.*

From the Latin *vapidus* meaning "flat, insipid." Originally this word was used to describe drinks lacking in flavor.

succulent *(adj.)* səkyələnt
Juicy and tender.

The restaurant was renowned for its **succulent** *steaks.*

Comes from the Latin for "juice." A succulent plant isn't one that we eat but one that lives in arid environments and retains a lot of moisture in its leaves.

briny *(adj.)* brīnē
Salty.

acrid *(adj.)* akrid
Bitter.

toothsome *(adj.)*
ˈto͞oTHsəm
Delicious.

palatable *(adj.)* palətəbəl
Pleasant-tasting, agreeable.

ACTIVITY 66

Complete the word for the missing definition:

1. salty = b__ny

2. bitter = _c_id

3. delicious = t___hs__e

4. lacking flavor, dull and uninteresting = i_si_i_

5. pleasant-tasting, agreeable = _al_t_b_e

6. juicy and tender = __cc_l__t

Fun

Expressing our amusement—or lack of it—these words take us from bored to bubbly.

ennui *(n.)* änˈwē
Lack of stimulation and excitement.

*The newly married couple could not handle the **ennui** of the suburbs and soon moved back to the city center.*

Though this word comes from eighteenth-century French, it originates from the Latin for "it is hateful to me." Even though the *y* is not pronounced, a good way to remember this word is to think of it as "yawn-we."

stultifying *(adj.)* stəltəˌfīˌNG
Lacking excitement because of tediousness.

*Dmitri was excited to start work at a major financial firm, but after a month of nothing but data entry, he found the job **stultifying**.*

From the Latin for "foolish." Think of this word as a combination of *boring* and *numbing*.

effervescent *(adj.)* efərˈves(ə)nt
Full of energy and liveliness.

*Harry was already energetic—after two cups of coffee he was downright **effervescent**.*

This word comes from the Latin for "boiling." *Effervescent* also describes a liquid that is bubbling and fizzy.

diversion *(n.)* dəˈvərZHən
A side entertainment or recreation.

buoyant *(adj.)* boiənt
Upbeat and optimistic.

avocation *(n.)*
avəˈkāSH(ə)n
A hobby.

ACTIVITY 67

Write the word that completes each sentence:

1. He was _____, practically bouncing off the walls.

2. Despite a struggling economy, the investors have remained _____ and expect to make a huge profit.

3. Most people have at least one _____ to pass the time while not working. (2 possible answers)

4. Working on an assembly line day in and day out can be _____.

5. As summer break neared and the teacher had little left for the students to learn, an _____ descended upon the classroom.

False Friends (PART 1)

Some words might have familiar-looking roots or even words in them, but the actual definition is not what you think. Because these words deviate from their original roots, their histories have been omitted.

insufferable *(adj.)* insəf(ə)rəb(ə)l
Conceited, stuck-up.

*Larry was **insufferable** during trivia games, constantly reminding his teammates how much he knew.*

The first known use of this word was in the early fifteenth century, meaning "not able to be suffered." While one definition of this word means "intolerable," the other definition (not relating to the original root) is the one focused on here.

unconscionable *(adj.)* ənˈkänSH(ə)nəbəl
Highly objectionable, unthinkable.

*The rogue government's actions were **unconscionable** to the point that some claimed that genocide was taking place.*

This word does not relate to consciousness, but rather *conscience*, or knowing the difference between what is right and wrong.

impertinent *(adj.)* imˈpərtnənt
Rude and poorly mannered.

*In many countries, it is considered **impertinent** to cut in line.*

Impertinent can also mean "not pertinent," however, this usage is far less common.

immaterial *(adj.)*
i(m)məˈtirēəl
Not relevant.

inflammable *(adj.)*
inflaməb(ə)l
Easily catching fire, flammable.

unnerve *(v.)* ənˈnərv
To frighten or cause one to lose confidence.

cogent *(adj.)* kōjənt
Clear and persuasive.

ACTIVITY 68

Mark "S" if the meanings of the two words are similar, "O" if they are opposite, or "D" if they are different:

1. flammable and inflammable _____

2. cogent and unconscionable _____

3. insufferable and impertinent _____

4. unnerve and immaterial _____

False Friends (PART 2)

buttress *(v.)* bətrəs
To provide support for (a building) or to reinforce or strengthen an idea.

*The theory was **buttressed** by years of clinical research.*

Not related to something you sit on.

garish *(adj.)* geriSH
Flashy in a cheap way.

*The **garish** jewelry—fake gold necklaces and silver rings—was part of his onstage persona.*

This word is not related to garrulous (talkative).

hapless *(adj.)* hapləs
Unfortunate, unlucky.

*He was a **hapless** gambler at the racetrack, losing everything on a single, unlucky bet.*

Hapless does not relate to happiness.

panache *(n.)* pəˈnaSH
Style, flair.

protean *(adj.)* prōdēən
Able to take on many different forms.

fatuous *(adj.)* faCHo͞oəs
Silly and idiotic.

ACTIVITY 69

Write the word that completes each sentence:

1. Throughout his career the actor has been _____, able to adapt to almost any role.

2. The comment was _____ because it added nothing and was quite silly.

3. The pianist plays with _____, often lifting his hands high in the air and having them land just in time.

4. The medicine's efficacy was _____ by numerous clinical studies.

5. Gary seems generally _____, as one bad thing after another happens to him.

6. The downtown area was lit up with 1,000 flashing neon lights, giving a _____ appearance.

Color Words

We all know our yellow from our green, our blue from our red. But there are other far less common color words that also pop up in English.

cerulean *(adj.)* səˈro͞olēən
Sky blue.

*Her eyes were light green, but the colored contact lenses made them appear **cerulean**.*

From the Latin for "sky blue." The cerulean warbler is a small songbird that is colored (you guessed it!) cerulean.

chartreuse *(adj.)* SHärˈtro͞oz
Yellowish green.

*The stained-glass windows were a mix of **chartreuse** and burgundy.*

Chartreuse comes from the name of a liqueur made in a French monastery. The highest quality chartreuse was a pale, apple green.

mauve *(adj.)* mōv, môv
Pale purple.

*In the morning light, the clouds dotting the horizon were little daubs of **mauve**.*

Originally from the Latin for "mallow," a plant with purple flowers.

azure *(adj.)* aZHər
Bright blue (similar to cerulean).

alabaster *(adj.)* aləˌbastər
Pale white, with a translucent appearance (can be used to describe skin).

taupe *(adj.)* tōp
Grayish brown.

puce *(adj.)* pyo͞os
Dark reddish-purple (like an eggplant).

ACTIVITY 70

Match the word with its definition:

1. taupe _____
2. azure _____
3. alabaster _____
4. chartreuse _____
5. cerulean _____
6. mauve _____
7. puce _____

a. pale white
b. sky blue
c. bright blue
d. reddish purple
e. grayish brown
f. pale purple
g. yellowish green

Colorful Words

This lesson features common colors that take on a different definition when combined with words that simply describe colorful people.

maroon *(v.)* məˈrōon
To abandon in an isolated place.

*He found himself **marooned** in the middle of Manhattan, his wallet missing and his family thousands of miles away.*

This word comes from the French for "chestnut." The color maroon is brownish red.

flamboyant *(adj.)* flamˈboi(y)ənt
Describing showy behavior that tries to attract attention.

*The rock star was known for his **flamboyant** attire, wearing a purple leather suit, green-tinted glasses, and a top hat covered in diamonds.*

From the French for "flaming." *Flamboyance* is the noun form of the word.

blackball *(v.)* blakˌbôl
To ban someone from a group or organization by means of a secret vote.

*After giving a speech while intoxicated, Barney was **blackballed** from the group of teetotalers.*

This word comes from an eighteenth-century voting procedure in which a black ball was placed in a ballot box to signal a nay vote. This word is similar to *blacklist*, which is a list (either literal or figurative) of those who have been rejected or barred from a group or organization.

blue *(adj.)* blōo
Depressed, sad.

outlandish *(adj.)*
outˈlandiSH
Bizarre in appearance or behavior.

ruddy *(adj.)* rədē
Red, usually when describing a person's face.

purple *(adj.)* pərpəl
Describing writing that tries to be too elaborate and fancy.

cynosure *(n.)*
sīnəˌSHŏo(ə)r
The center of attention, whether a person or thing.

ACTIVITY 71

Write the word that completes each sentence:

1. When it was cold outside, his face became _____, and his friend joked that he looked like a beardless Santa.

2. The editor omitted large sections of the prose that were too _____.

Complete the word for each definition:

3. the center of attention = _yn__ure

4. to ban someone from a group or organization by means of a secret vote = __ackba___

5. describing showy behavior that tries to attract attention = _la_b__ant

Spending Words

Whether you pinch pennies or spend money as soon as you get it, the words below will have you covered.

frugal *(adj.)* frо̄o͞ogəl
Wise with money, thrifty.

*She only had a tiny amount of money to spend each week so was forced to be **frugal**.*

From the Latin for "fruit." The noun form of the word is *frugality*.

magnanimous *(adj.)* magˈnanəməs
Generous and kind, likely to forgive.

*Despite the fact that his son had squandered his money, the father remained **magnanimous** and continued to believe that his son would one day become frugal.*

Comes from the Latin for "large spirit." Though it doesn't really roll off the tongue very easily, it is good to know that the noun form of this word is *magnanimity*.

munificent *(adj.)* myо̄o͞oˈnifəsənt
Very generous and giving.

*The aunt was **munificent**, providing large sums to pay for the tuition for her three nieces.*

From the Latin *munus-* meaning "gift." The noun form—*munificence*—is a synonym of the word *largesse*.

miserly *(adj.)* mīzərlē
Penny pinching.

parsimonious *(adj.)*
pärsəˈmōnēəs
Miserly.

largesse *(n.)* lorˈZHes
Generosity in giving gifts, or the actual gift itself.

economical *(adj.)*
ekəˈnämik(ə)l
Frugal, not using more than is necessary.

ACTIVITY 72

Write the word that completes each sentence:

1. Their grandfather was _____ throughout his life, always buying what was cheapest. (3 possible answers)

2. Her writing was _____, never employing an unneeded word.

3. Grandma was generally frugal, but come Christmas time she was known for her _____, showering gifts on the entire family. (2 possible answers)

4. Despite all the times her younger brother had let her down, Sheila was _____ and never held a grudge against him.

Let's Party

Some make the pursuit of pleasure a lifestyle. Others simply overdo it.

hedonist (n.) hēdənəst
One who pursues pleasure as the main goal in life.

*The music festival was a **hedonist**'s dream: a three-day party on white sand beaches.*

From a Greek school of thought that the pursuit of pleasure is the meaning of life. An antonym to hedonist is *ascetic*.

prodigal (adj.) prädəgəl
Spending money recklessly.

*Without good financial planning, some celebrities become **prodigal**, squandering millions in a matter of years.*

From the Latin for "lavish." Many familiar with the Bible know this word because of the story of the prodigal son, who squandered his money on a life of gambling and lavishness.

sybarite (n.) sibə͵rīt
A person who indulges in highly luxurious and sensual things.

*A **sybarite** could easily spend all day at a spa, getting one luxurious treatment after another.*

From an ancient city in Greece—Sybaris—where the inhabitants devoted themselves to a life of luxury. The adjective form of this word is *sybaritic*.

spendthrift (n.)
spen(d)͵THrift
A person who wastes money.

profligate (adj.) präfləgət
Extremely wasteful with resources (not just money).

epicurean (adj.)
epəkyəˈrēən
Devoted to a life of pleasure but with a tendency for the refined.

ACTIVITY 73

Write the word that completes each sentence:

1. He might not be a _____, but he certainly liked to pamper himself at the spa from time to time. (2 possible answers)

2. The government was _____, driving up the national debt even higher. (2 possible answers)

3. Many rock star biographies follow a similar narrative arc—years of _____ behavior and wild living followed by years of quiet reflection.

4. He was a true _____ and could never seem to hold on to his money.

Words from the Body

Our bodies have begotten a surprising number of words that have interesting secondary definitions.

hamstring *(v.)* ham͵striNG
To make powerless.

*The committee was **hamstrung** by severe budget cuts and unable to institute many of the planned changes.*

This word is derived from the tendon in the back of the knee; when it was cut, the person or animal would be unable to walk. The past tense of this word is *hamstrung*, not *hamstringed*, the latter of which is not a word.

aquiline *(adj.)* akwə͵līn
Describing a person's nose that is hooked like an eagle's beak.

*Despite his prominent **aquiline** nose, the actor was still seen as a heartthrob.*

From the Latin for "eagle." Technically this word is not from our body, but describes a part of our body.

sanguine *(adj.)* saNGgwən
Cheerfully optimistic.

*With the sudden economic downturn, recent college grads are not **sanguine** about their job prospects.*

From the Latin for "blood"; it was thought that when someone was optimistic, blood rushed to their cheeks. Like *choleric* and *bilious*, this word comes from the "humors," bodily fluids the Greeks imagined coursed through our body. Their specific balance resulted in personality traits. The fourth humor, phlegm, gives us the word *phlegmatic*.

choleric *(adj.)* kälərik
Easily angered.

bilious *(adj.)* ˈbilyəs
Bad tempered.

sartorial *(adj.)*
särˈtôrēəl
Relating to a tailor or tailored clothes.

ACTIVITY 74

Mark "S" if the meanings of the two words are similar, "R" if they are related, and "NR" if they are not related:

1. sartorial and hamstring _____

2. bilious and choleric _____

3. sanguine and sartorial _____

4. aquiline and hamstring _____

Words from Myth

Greek mythology is a rich source of many interesting English words.

narcissist *(n.)* närsəsəst
One overly concerned with the way one looks or is perceived.

*He is a **narcissist** and will spend hours in his room taking selfies, looking for the perfect angle.*

In Greek myth, Narcissus was a young man so taken with the beauty of his own reflection in a pond that he fell headfirst into the water. Narcissism is also a psychological disorder in which a person is so obsessed with themselves that they have difficulty forming genuine connections with others.

herculean *(adj.)* hərkyəˈlēən
Requiring great effort.

*For many, it required **herculean** effort not to return for a second helping of the delicious cheesecake.*

From Hercules, the Greek demigod known for his great strength. This word can also mean "very strong," but this definition is not as common.

chimera *(n.)* kīˈmirə, kəˈmirə
An illusion or unattainable idea.

*Achieving speed-of-light travel, despite what the movies tell you, is a **chimera**.*

In Greek myth, the Chimera was a monster with a lion's head, goat's body, and serpent's tail. Two common phrases that are similar to chimera are *pipe dream* and *castle in the air.*

elysian *(adj.)* iˈliZH(ē)ən
Like paradise.

apollonian *(adj.)* apəˈlōnēən
Relating to people's rational side.

dionysian *(adj.)* dīəˈnisēən
Relating to people's emotional side.

ACTIVITY 75

Provide the word for the given definition:

1. like paradise = _____

2. relating to people's emotional side = _____

3. relating to people's rational side = _____

4. one overly consumed with the way one looks or is perceived = _____

5. an illusion or unattainable idea = _____

6. requiring great effort = _____

Heavenly Words

Whether we look up to the skies for literal or figurative inspiration, the heavens have long given us light—plus a few "divine" words to add to our list.

cherub *(n.)* CHerəb
A healthy young child or baby with an angelic appearance.

*With his round, pink cheeks and locks of golden hair, the little boy resembled a **cherub**.*

This word comes from the Hebrew and describes the second-highest ranking of the angels in the Bible, below the seraphim. Cherubs are found throughout European art, and are often mistaken for plump babies, rather than angels.

sublime *(adj.)* səˈblīm
Glorious, exalted.

*Mozart's piano concerti are **sublime**, as though a higher being had dictated the notes to the composer.*

From the Latin for "up to the threshold"—presumably of heaven. Root-wise, *sublime* is related to *subliminal*, which describes something that our minds are completely aware of, though today the words have very different meanings.

cosmogony *(n.)* käzˈmägənē
The study of and theories about the origins of the universe.

*The **cosmogony** of ancient people differed greatly from the modern notion of a "big bang."*

From the Greek *kosmos-* ("world") and *-gony* ("creation"). When you hear physicists (or, for that matter, anyone) discussing the Big Bang Theory, they are discussing *cosmogony*.

ethereal *(adj.)*
əˈTHirēəl
Heavenly.

seraphic *(adj.)* səˈrafik
Describing somebody with an angelic appearance.

theodicy *(n.)* THēˈädəsē
The belief that all the evil in the world has some divine, higher purpose.

empyrean *(n.)* emˈpirēən
The heavens, sky.

numinous *(adj.)*
n(y)o͞omənəs
Supernatural.

ACTIVITY 76

Provide the word for the given definition:

1. the study of and theories about the origins of the universe = _____

2. glorious, exalted = _____

3. supernatural = _____

4. the belief that all the evil in the world has some divine, higher purpose = _____

5. a baby with an angelic appearance = _____

6. describing somebody with an angelic appearance = _____

Two-Faced Words

The English language possesses some very confusing words named after the Greek god Janus, he of two faces: one sad and the other happy. The following words are examples of such two-faced words, with dual definitions that are almost opposite of each other.

cleave *(v.)* klēv
To split apart *or* to hold closer together.

*The cook used the large knife to **cleave** the meat from the bone.*

*The child **cleaved** to his mother's chest as they made their way over the mountain pass.*

sanction *(v.)* saNG(k)SHən
To penalize, punish *or* to allow, authorize.

*The rogue regime was **sanctioned** by trade embargos from neighboring countries hoping to force the dictator out of power.*

*There is only one specific game ball **sanctioned** by FIFA, soccer's governing body.*

Interestingly, the *sanction* used is often determined by whether the context is domestic or international.

buckle *(v.)* bəkəl
To fasten *or* to collapse.

*The racecar drivers **buckled** their belt harnesses to protect them in the event of a crash.*

*The bridge began to **buckle** under the constant weight of thousands of cars each day.*

re-sign/resign *(v.)* riˈzīn
To sign again *or* to quit.

*The star **re-signed** his contract with the championship-winning team.*

*The CFO **resigned** after it had been leaked to the media that he'd embezzled funds.*

Interestingly, to be resigned is to accept something that one doesn't necessarily like (e.g., he was resigned to his fate).

ACTIVITY 77

Mark "T" for true and "F" for false:

1. *buckle* can mean "to secure" or "to collapse" _____

2. *resign* can mean "to accept something unpleasant" or "to sign again" _____

3. *sanction* can mean "to prohibit" or "to allow" _____

4. *cleave* can mean "to enter" or "to depart" _____

A Matter of Trust

Whether you are generally trustworthy or wary of other's intentions, English has many words expressing how easily you are duped or how adept you are at deceiving others.

naïve *(adj.)* nī´ēv
Lacking in worldly experience, innocent of the true ways of the world.

*When the scammer called telling him he'd won a prize, Chester **naïvely** coughed up his credit card number.*

From the Latin for "natural." The symbol of two dots over the letter *i* in *naïve* is called a dieresis and is used to show that there is a break between the pronunciation of the vowels *i* and *a*.

ingenuous *(adj.)* ˌinˈjenyo͞oəs
Unaware, innocent, unpretentious.

*She was **ingenuous** at times, thinking that everyone was good at heart and no one would ever lie to her.*

Comes from the Latin for "native" and "inborn," suggesting youth and lack of experience. This word is a combination of *trusting* and *childlike*.

subterfuge *(n.)* səbtərˌfyo͞oj
Deception and trickery for a specific purpose.

*The spy's **subterfuge** was elaborate; she lied to countless others about her origins to get closer to her target.*

This word comes from the Latin *sub-* ("below") and *fug-* ("to escape"). *Subterfuge* is a synonym of *duplicity*.

conniving *(adj.)* kəˈnīviNG
Scheming and conspiring to do ill.

disingenuous *(adj.)*
ˌdisinˈjenyəwəs
Pretending to be innocent and honest but actually knowing more than one acknowledges.

duplicity *(n.)*
d(y)o͞oˈplisədē
Deceit, putting on a false face.

mendacious *(adj.)*
menˈdāSHəs
Not telling the truth.

legerdemain *(n.)*
lejərdəˌmān
Sleight of hand, deception.

ACTIVITY 78

Mark "S" if the meanings of the two words are similar, "O" if they are opposite, or "D" if they are different:

1. mendacious and duplicitous _____

2. subterfuge and ingenuous _____

3. disingenuous and conniving _____

4. naïve and legerdemain _____

How Much Do You Know?

Some seem to know everything, while others struggle to remember where they placed their keys.

savant *(n.)* saˈvän(t)
A respected thinker and scholar.

*In the 1940s, Princeton was crawling with **savants**—Einstein and Oppenheimer, to name a few.*

From the French for "knowing." A *savant* can describe a person who thrives at feats of memory while otherwise exhibiting intellectual disability.

neophyte *(n.)* nēəˌfīt
A person who is new to learning something.

*She was a Microsoft Excel **neophyte** one day, fiddling with simple equations, and a virtual savant the next, working pivot tables.*

This comes from the Latin for "newly planted." This word originally was used to describe those who were new to a religious order. Today, the word *novitiate* is more common when describing such a person.

polymath *(n.)* pälēˌmaTH
One who is learned in a variety of different fields.

*Mike was a true **polymath**, able to talk about medieval history one moment and quantum physics the next.*

From the Greek *poly-* for "much" and *math-* for "knowledge." The *-math* root pops up in the not-too-common word *opsimath*, which describes a person who learns something late in life.

novice *(n.)* nävəs
Beginner.

maven *(n.)* māvən
An expert.

greenhorn *(n.)* grēnˌhôrn
A person new to a field of learning or activity.

sagacious *(adj.)*
səˈgāSHəs
Wise and clever.

tyro *(n.)* tīrō
A person who is new to something.

ACTIVITY 79

Write the word that completes each sentence:

1. She was a _____, having triple-majored in college and picked up three graduate degrees.

2. He was a self-described fashion _____, and his friends often consulted him for his expertise on the latest fads.

Unscramble the word and define:

3. tory _____

4. vansat _____

5. ivcone _____

6. gonererhn _____

Money, Money, Money

The following words cover the richest to the poorest and relate in general to the acquisition of money.

destitute *(adj.)* destə͵t(y)o͞ot
Not having the basic needs in life.

*After the flood, the family was left **destitute**, their home no longer livable and their many belongings unsalvageable.*

From the Latin for "deserted and abandoned." Synonyms include *impoverished* and *penniless*.

affluent *(adj.)* aflo͞oənt
Wealthy.

*The homes perched on the hilltop represent the city's **affluent** community.*

This word comes from the Latin for "flowing freely." This word is often coupled with *communities* or *areas*.

cupidity *(n.)* kyo͞o'pidədē
Excessive greed for money.

*He would do anything for money, his **cupidity** knowing no bounds.*

From the Latin for "desire." We associate Cupid with love, not with money. Yet, cupidity and Cupid are similar in terms of desire.

lavish *(adj.)* laviSH
Luxurious and costly in appearance.

opulent *(adj.)* äpyələnt
Suggesting great wealth and luxury (describing a place).

avarice *(n.)* avərəs
Greed.

penurious *(adj.)*
pə'n(y)o͞orēəs
Impoverished or stingy.

impecunious *(adj.)*
impə'kyo͞onēəs
Poor.

ACTIVITY 80

Write the word that completes each sentence:

1. The five-star hotel is truly _____, its lobby fringed with actual gold. (2 possible answers)

2. Many driven by _____ invested thousands of dollars, hoping to make millions. (2 possible answers)

3. His was a true rags-to-riches story, going from being _____ to being _____.

4. The brochures depicted _____ accommodations ("fit for a king"), though in reality the hotel was run-down and nothing like the pictures. (2 possible answers)

Political Words (PART 1)

The world of politics has given us a bounty of intriguing words.

muckraker *(n.)* ˈmək͵rākər
Writer whose work exposes corruption in business or politics.

*As long as there is duplicity in politics, there will be **muckrakers** with pens.*

This word comes from *Pilgrim's Progress*, a seventeenth-century literary work describing one who rakes filth. Later Theodore Roosevelt used this term to describe those journalists who expose corruption in society. A *muckraker* is another way of saying investigative journalist.

incumbent *(n.)* inˈkəmbənt
One currently holding a political office.

*In the United States, a sitting president can be reelected as an **incumbent** only once, since no president can serve more than two terms.*

From the Latin to "lie on top." As an adjective, *incumbent* has a secondary meaning, describing a duty or responsibility that is necessary for someone to do.

gerrymander *(v.)* jerēˌmandər
To break up political boundaries in an odd shape in order to give oneself or one's party an electoral edge.

*The only way the incumbent can get reelected is if they seriously **gerrymander** the place.*

Named after Vice President Elbridge Gerry, who divided up his district in Massachusetts into electoral zones that would ensure his victory. The resulting shape happened to be similar to that of a salamander.

canvass *(v.)* kanvəs
To go about (usually on foot) asking for people's votes.

inaugurate *(v.)*
iˈnôg(y)əˌrāt
To signal, usually with a ceremony, the beginning of a person's term.

barnstorm *(v.)*
bärnˌstôrm
To make a rapid tour through rural areas for the purpose of acquiring votes.

mudslinging *(n.)*
mədˌsliNGiNG
The act of insulting or defaming a political opponent.

interregnum *(v.)*
in(t)ərˈregnəm
The period between one ruler leaving office and another taking over, or a slight pause in the government if a person in power is voted in for another term.

ACTIVITY 81

Match the word with its meaning:

1. barnstorm _____
2. interregnum _____
3. incumbent _____
4. mudslinging _____
5. inaugurate _____
6. canvass _____

a. the act of insulting or defaming a political opponent
b. to signal the beginning of a person's term in office
c. to go about asking for people's votes
d. one currently holding a political office
e. the period between one ruler leaving office and another taking over
f. to make a rapid tour through rural areas for the purpose of acquiring votes

Political Words (PART 2)

partisan *(n.)* ˈpärtəzən
One loyal to a group or a political party.

*He had been a **partisan** of the Democratic Party for years but now identifies as an Independent.*

From the Latin for "part." A *nonpartisan* is one who tries to refrain from supporting any one party.

filibuster *(v.)* filəˌbəstər
To engage in deliberate stalling practices so that a vote on a measure cannot take place.

*To prevent the vote to close the old lumber mill from taking place, the committee of lumberjacks **filibustered**.*

This comes from the word for "freebooter," or a pirate. The most common form of filibustering is perhaps the giving of really long speeches (13 hours is not uncommon).

demagogue *(n.)* deməˌgäg
A leader who manipulates the public's emotions for his or her own ends.

***Demagogues** tend to be gifted orators who can rouse a crowd's emotions.*

From the Greek for "people" and "leading." To engage in these kinds of practices is to engage in demagoguery.

lame duck *(n.)* lām ˈdək
A president who, after the election of his successor, spends his time in office ineffectually.

politico *(n.)* pəˈlidikō
Politician.

apparatchik *(n.)*
äpəˈräCHik
A blindly loyal official in an (often political) organization.

plenary *(adj.)* plenərē
Describing a session attended by all members of a governing body.

ACTIVITY 82

Match the word with its definition:

1. politico _____

2. plenary _____

3. filibuster _____

4. demagogue _____

5. lame duck _____

6. partisan _____

7. apparatchik _____

a. to delay in deliberate stalling practices so that a vote on a measure cannot take place

b. a leader who manipulates the public's emotions for his or her own ends

c. a president who, after the election of his successor, spends his time in office ineffectually

d. a blindly loyal official in an (often political) organization

e. one loyal to a political party

f. politician

g. describing a session attended by all members of a governing body

It's a Rebellion!

To start a rebellion or to squash one, these words have you covered.

insurrection *(n.)* insəˈrekSH(ə)n
A violent revolution against a ruling body.

*The **insurrections** removed power from the King, thereby ending 40 years of oppressive rule.*

From the Latin for "to rise up." *Uprising* is a synonym for *insurrection*.

quell *(v.)* kwel
To put an end to unrest or insurrection, to suppress.

*Once the prime minister realized there was no way to **quell** the riots, he fled the country.*

From the Old English for "to kill" or the German for "to torture." Good synonyms are *squash*, *quash*, and *subdue*.

foment *(v.)* fōˈment
To stir up rebellion.

*Once the royal guard identified the person responsible for **fomenting** rebellion, the riots stopped overnight.*

This comes from the Latin for "to heat." *Instigate* and *agitate* are two good synonyms.

insurgency *(n.)* inˈsərj(ə)nsē
An ongoing revolt or insurrection.

agitate *(v.)* ajəˌtāt
To incite a riot or cause a group to act violently.

seditious *(adj.)* səˈdiSHəs
Describing behavior or action intended to stir up a revolt.

subversive *(adj.)* səbˈvərsiv
Aimed at upsetting the current order.

ACTIVITY 83

Mark "S" if the meanings of the two words are similar, "O" if they are opposite, or "D" if they are different:

1. seditious and subversive _____

2. quell and foment _____

3. insurgency and insurrection _____

4. subdue and agitate _____

Biblical Words

The Bible has provided us with many noteworthy vocabulary words.

advent *(n.)* adˌvent
The beginning of a major event or phenomenon.

*With the **advent** of television, the dominance of radio ended seemingly overnight.*

From the Latin for "arrival." In Christianity, this word describes the month leading up to Christmas.

scapegoat *(n.)* skāpˌgōt
A person or thing blamed for an offense it did not commit.

*Though Timmy was the one who ate the entire package of cookies, his two-year-old brother made for a convenient **scapegoat**.*

This was from the book of Leviticus of the Old Testament, describing a goat that "carried" the sins of all the people and was cast into the forest. A colloquial phrase that has a similar meaning is "whipping boy."

epiphany *(n.)* əˈpifənē
A sudden realization or insight.

*After years working in a large corporation, Carla had an **epiphany** that she wanted to start her own business.*

From the Greek for "to reveal." This is also a Christian celebration, starting on January 6, that commemorates Jesus appearing before the Gentiles.

idolatry *(n.)* īˈdälətrē
The worship of idols.

atonement *(n.)* əˈtōnmənt
The making of amends for wrongdoing.

pestilence *(n.)* pestələns
A widespread disease.

leviathan *(n.)* ləˈvīəθən
A large beast, or figuratively any large organization that wields great power.

ACTIVITY 84

Write the word that completes each sentence:

1. The tech _____ has become so powerful that it affects how people lead their lives.

2. A _____ had swept through the southern part of the country, leaving many sick and some dead.

3. For missing their anniversary for three years running, Michael's _____ was to cook dinner for his wife for an entire month.

4. The _____ of the smartphone has fundamentally changed the way we communicate with others.

What's the Big Joke?

We all like to laugh. But there is more than one way of laughing. Humor has a spectrum of subtlety, so here are just a few terms to help describe what makes you chuckle.

chortle *(v.)* CHôrtl
To laugh merrily and nasally.

*Taking a sip of tea, he **chortled** at her joke, spilling some of his drink.*

From Lewis Carroll's *Through the Looking-Glass,* this word is a portmanteau of chuckle and snort. Lewis Carroll was fond of portmanteaus, coming up with a nonsense poem— "Jabberwocky"—that was full of them.

irreverent *(adj.)* iˈrev(ə)rənt
Not showing respect during occasions that call for seriousness.

*Just as the esteemed speaker was getting to the moral of his story, someone in the audience let out an **irreverent** laugh.*

This word comes from the opposite of *revere*, or "to respect deeply." The noun form is *irreverence*.

sardonic *(adj.)* särˈdänik
Bitingly sarcastic and mocking, sneering.

*At the height of the crisis, the mayor tried to reassure the crowd that everything was fine, when one of his detractors bleated **sardonically**, "We've heard that before."*

From Homer's time, this word comes from a description of the residents of Sardinia. Make sure not to treat this word as interchangeable with *sarcastic*. *Sardonic* is a harsher form of *sarcastic*.

parody *(n.)* parədē
An exaggerated imitation of something or someone for comic effect.

guffaw *(v.)* gəˈfô
A loud, unrestrained laugh.

wry *(adj.)* rī
Dryly sarcastic.

uproarious *(adj.)*
əpˈrôˊrēəs
Extremely funny.

flippant *(adj.)* flipənt
Not showing proper respect, irreverent.

ACTIVITY 85

Match the word with its definition:

1. flippant _____
2. parody _____
3. sardonic _____
4. uproarious _____
5. guffaw _____
6. wry _____

a. a loud, unrestrained laugh

b. extremely funny

c. not showing proper respect, irreverent

d. bitingly sarcastic

e. dryly sarcastic

f. an exaggerated imitation for comic effect

It's No Laughing Matter

What would laughter be without words to express the opposite? For moments of deep sadness or simply dignified behavior, the words below are nothing to laugh at.

grave *(adj.)* grāv
Extremely serious.

*His expression was **grave** when he reported the people who'd gone missing.*

From the Latin for "heavy, serious." Good synonyms are *somber* and *grim*.

lament *(v.)* lə'ment
To mourn and wail, or to express deep regret.

*As an old man, he **lamented** all the opportunities he'd wasted while younger.*

This comes from the Latin for "wailing." *Rue* and *bemoan* are two good synonyms to know.

decorum *(n.)* də'kôrəm
The proper behavior or conduct, typically in a formal context.

*He ignored typical rules of **decorum** by wearing a T-shirt and jeans to the wedding.*

From the Latin for "appropriate." The word *indecorous* is an adjective meaning "lacking decorum."

dirge *(n.)* dərj
A song usually accompanying a funeral.

propriety *(n.)*
p(r)ə'prīədē
Proper behavior or conduct.

disconsolate *(adj.)*
dis'käns(ə)lət
So sad that one cannot be consoled or made happy.

elegiac *(adj.)* elə'jīək
Extremely mournful.

ACTIVITY 86

Mark "S" if the meanings of the two words are similar, "O" if they are opposite, or "D" if they are different:

1. morose and disconsolate _____

2. propriety and decorum _____

3. dirge and lament _____

Recognition

Whether you are the most famous face on the planet or a person rarely recognized, these words have got you covered.

obscure *(adj.)* əbˈskyo͞or
Not well known.

*Even the most famous of actors was once an **obscure** thespian hoping to make it big.*

From the Latin for "dark." *Obscure* can also describe knowledge that few possess; in this sense, a synonym is *esoteric*.

illustrious *(adj.)* iˈləstrēəs
Well known, famous for positive achievements.

*She was one of the most **illustrious** figures in Hollywood during the 1940s, known by all.*

This word comes from the Latin for "bright." *Eminent* and *prominent* are two synonyms for *illustrious*.

nonentity *(n.)* näˈnen(t)ədē
An unknown person, one lacking in importance.

*As the new kid, he felt like a **nonentity** for the first few months until he finally established his circle of friends.*

From the Latin for "nonexistence." A *nobody* or a *zero* is another way to think of *nonentity*.

notoriety *(n.)* nōdəˈrīədē
A bad reputation.

fanfare *(n.)* fanfer
Attention and adulation typically accompanying a famous person.

snub *(v.)* snəb
To ignore, pass over.

cipher *(n.)* sīfər
A person of no importance.

ACTIVITY 87

Mark "S" if the meanings of the two words are similar, "O" if they are opposite, or "D" if they are different:

1. cipher and nonentity _____

2. snub and illustrious _____

3. nonentity and obscure _____

Write the word that completes each sentence:

4. Though she had waited the entire evening to see him, she felt _____ when he looked away from her.

5. Everywhere the Beatles went in the 1960s, they were greeted with _____.

Make Up Your Mind

Can't make up your mind, or do you just go with the flow?

irresolute *(adj.)* i(r)ˈrezəˌlo͞ot
Unable to make up one's mind.

*When it came to choosing majors, he was **irresolute**, unable to choose between physics and music until his second year.*

From Latin for "not loose." *Vacillate* is a verb meaning to go back and forth between two options—something one who is irresolute is likely to do.

obdurate *(adj.)* äbd(y)ərət
Stubborn and not willing to change one's mind.

*The **obdurate** child refused to get out of bed and get ready for school.*

From the Latin for "hardened into sin," this word has lost the connotation of wrongdoing, and now simply means "stubborn." *Mulish*, a word from an earlier lesson, is a good synonym for this word.

acquiesce *(v.)* akwēˈes
To give in, albeit reluctantly.

*Though Jill really didn't want to watch the latest horror flick, her friends kept pestering her until she finally **acquiesced**.*

This comes from the Latin for "to rest at." The noun form of this word is *acquiescence*.

insubordinate *(adj.)*
insəˈbôrd(ə)nət
Difficult to control, rebellious.

impressionable *(adj.)*
imˈpreSH(ə)nəb(ə)l
Easily influenced.

amenable *(adj.)*
əˈmēnəb(ə)l
Agreeable and likely to go along.

pliant *(adj.)* plīənt
Giving in easily to the will of others.

intransigent *(adj.)*
inˈtransəjənt
Unyielding, not budging in one's position.

ACTIVITY 88

Mark "S" if the meanings of the two words are similar, "O" if they are opposite, or "D" if they are different:

1. amenable and pliant _____

2. insubordinate and intransigent _____

3. obdurate and irresolute _____

Something Wicked This Way Comes

There are bad people, and there are nefarious people. There are also good people, and those who are irreproachable.

ruthless *(adj.)* rŌoTHləs
Having no compassion, merciless.

*The twentieth century was full of **ruthless** dictators who cared little for the lives of the people they ruled.*

From the archaic word *ruth*, which is related to *rue*, meaning "to regret." *Merciless* and *coldhearted* are two synonyms for *ruthless*.

scrupulous *(adj.)* skrŌopyələs
Acting according to morality and good conduct.

*He was a **scrupulous** driver, always driving below the speed limit and always coming to a complete stop at every stop sign.*

Derived from the word *scruple*, which in Latin meant "pebble," used as a metaphor for anxiety. *Scrupulous* has a second definition, meaning "paying careful attention to what one is doing."

nefarious *(adj.)* niˈfe(ə)rēəs
Extremely wicked and villainous.

*The movie featured a typical superhero, one who wanted to save the world from the **nefarious** plans of his nemesis.*

From the Latin for "wrong." Nefarious characters from movies include Norman Bates (from *Psycho*) and the Joker (from the *Batman* movies).

irreproachable *(adj.)*
iriˈprōCHəbəl
Without fault.

incorruptible *(adj.)*
inkəˈrəptəbəl
Not capable of being corrupted.

diabolical *(adj.)*
dīəˈbälikəl
Evil, like the devil.

turpitude *(n.)*
tərpiˌt(y)ōod
Extremely immoral behavior, depravity.

ACTIVITY 89

Write the word that completes each sentence:

1. The candidate seemed _____, and no matter how hard his opponents tried to dig for dirt, they came up short.

2. Throughout his career the judge would not accept bribes and was therefore considered _____.

3. The man was publicly condemned for his _____, and many believed that his actions were so immoral that he simply could not atone.

4. He was _____ through and through, never once telling a lie.

5. The killer was _____, showing no mercy to his victims.

Are You the Boss or the Bossed?

Are you the one in charge? Or perhaps you are climbing the ladder of respect and power? Learn some colorful words that address these topics.

kowtow *(v.)* kouˈtou
To show meek and subservient behavior.

*The new employee **kowtowed** to upper management at every opportunity.*

This comes from the Chinese for "to knock head"; it originally referred to deferentially touching one's head to the ground. This word is used more generally to describe any meek and subservient behavior.

imperious *(adj.)* imˈpi(ə)rēəs
Extremely bossy and commanding, often without basis.

*The new chef, despite being less skillful than some of his staff, was **imperious**, barking out instructions to everyone in the kitchen.*

From the Latin for "command." *Dictatorial* and *domineering* are two good synonyms.

supercilious *(adj.)* so͞opərˈsilēəs
Looking down at others disdainfully.

*Now a multimillionaire and no longer a scrawny teen, Philip went to his high school class reunion and eyed his former classmates with a **supercilious** expression.*

From the word for "eyebrow," the definition comes from the fact that a disdainful look is often accompanied by an arched eyebrow. This word is synonymous with *haughty*.

deferential *(adj.)*
defəˈrenCHəl
Showing proper respect.

impudent *(adj.)*
impyəd(ə)nt
Cheeky and rude.

haughty *(adj.)* hôtē
Arrogant, believing oneself to be better than others.

peremptory *(adj.)*
pəˈremptərē
Bossy and domineering.

ACTIVITY 90

Mark "S" if the meanings of the two words are similar, "O" if they are opposite, or "D" if they are different:

1. supercilious and deferential _____

2. haughty and imperious _____

3. impudent and kowtow _____

4. peremptory and imperious _____

Commonly Confused Words

These words are often thought to mean something else—in some cases the very opposite of their definition.

nonplussed *(adj.)* nän'pləst
Confused to the point of not knowing how to act.

*The players became **nonplussed** when the basketball got wedged in the rim, and they had to wait for the ref to knock the ball free.*

From the Latin for "not more." Many people use this word incorrectly, thinking it means the exact opposite—calm, self-assured.

contrite *(adj.)* kən'trīt
Expressing remorse and experiencing guilt.

*The defendant was given a lighter sentence because he was **contrite**, openly weeping in court when recounting the night of the crime.*

This comes from Latin, meaning "grind down." This word is not related to *trite*, which describes an idea lacking originality. *Contrite* describes a person who feels guilty because of something he or she has done.

histrionic *(adj.)* histrē'änik
Melodramatic, hammy.

*The director's **histrionics** were infamous—when a scene didn't go quite the way he wanted, he would throw his chair, insult the actors, and often walk off the set.*

This comes from the Latin for "actor" and does not relate to history but theatrics.

confound *(v.)* kən'found
To confuse or bewilder or to regard two different things as if they were the same.

ponderous *(adj.)*
pändərəs
Moving with great difficulty.

ACTIVITY 91

Write the word for the given definition:

1. moving with great difficulty = _____

2. to confuse or bewilder = _____

3. confused to the point of not knowing how to act = _____

4. melodramatic = _____

5. remorseful = _____

Words from Yiddish

Yiddish is another language that has given English some particularly colorful words.

chutzpah *(n.)* hŏŏotspə
Nerve, effrontery.

*Even though the lecturer had politely asked the student to take his call outside, the student had the **chutzpah** to say it's too cold out there.*

From the Yiddish for "cheekiness, impudence." *Audacity* is a synonym for *chutzpah* and a good word to know.

klutz *(n.)* kləts
A clumsy person.

*Her cast and crutches turned her into a total **klutz**, knocking over things every few seconds.*

This word comes from the Yiddish for "wooden block." *Klutz* is typically used informally.

nebbish *(n.)* nebiSH
A meek, ineffectual person.

*He was such a **nebbish** that it was hard for him to get a date.*

From the Yiddish for "poor thing." Like *klutz*, this word is typically used informally.

schmaltzy *(adj.)*
SHmôltsē
Excessively sentimental.

kibitz *(v.)* kibits
To chat, speak informally with someone.

shtick *(n.)* SHtik
One's routine, typically in a comic setting or the style of a particular person.

kvetch *(v.)* kəˈveCH
To complain.

ACTIVITY 92

Write the word for the given definition:

1. one's comedic routine or the style of a particular person = _____

2. excessively sentimental = _____

3. to chat with someone = _____

4. a clumsy person = _____

5. nerve, effrontery = _____

6. to complain = _____

Words from Other Languages

English words are derived from a smattering of languages across the globe, including the following from Dutch, Turkish, Arabic, and more.

maelstrom *(n.)* mālˌsträm
A situation marked by chaotic movement.

*Black Friday was once again a **maelstrom** of shoppers crowding the entryway, hoping for the best deal.*

From early Dutch, this word describes a whirlpool that supposedly existed somewhere in the Atlantic. *Pandemonium* is a synonym for *maelstrom*.

bazaar *(n.)* bəˈzär
A marketplace, typically outdoors.

*She was able to find some exotic souvenirs at the **bazaar**.*

From the Turkish for "market." *Bazaar* can also describe a fundraising event in which goods are sold.

clairvoyant *(adj.)* klerˈvoiənt
Able to predict the future.

*The woman at the circus claimed to be **clairvoyant**, but her predictions were so generic that few believe she possessed such powers.*

This word comes from the French for "seeing clearly." Unlike *prescient*, which implies a good sense of what the future is likely to bring, *clairvoyant* literally means "being able to read the future."

saga *(n.)* sägə
A long, involved tale.

berserk *(adj.)* bərˈzərk
Out of control.

mecca *(n.)* mekə
A place that attracts many people.

hegira *(n.)* hejərə
A mass exodus.

ACTIVITY 93

Write the word for the given definition:

1. able to predict the future = _____

2. out of control = _____

3. a situation marked by chaotic movement = _____

4. a marketplace = _____

5. a place that attracts many people = _____

6. a mass exodus = _____

Order and Leveling

Whether describing the highest to the lowest, the first to the last, these words can come in handy.

mediocre *(adj.)* mēdē ˈōkər
So-so in quality, middle-of-the-road, not that great.

Steve's singing skills were **mediocre,** *but what he lacked in vocals he made up for in onstage pizzazz.*

From the Latin for "middle of a mountain." *Middling* and *lackluster* are two similar words.

cardinal *(adj.)* kärd(ə)nl
First in importance, fundamental.

The **cardinal** *rule of our support group is to let each person speak without interruption.*

This word comes from the Latin for "hinge." Cardinals are a group of top-ranking officials in the Roman Catholic church who elect the pope.

penultimate *(adj.)* pə ˈnəltəmət
Second to last.

Harold thought he didn't make the team, but to his relief, he ended up being the **penultimate** *player selected.*

From the Latin for "almost last." *Antepenultimate* is the word meaning "third to last," but it is rarely used.

abysmal *(adj.)* ə ˈbizməl
Extremely awful, really bad.

mundane *(adj.)*
mən ˈdān
Commonplace, uninteresting.

nonpareil *(adj.)* nänpə ˈrel
Without equal, unrivaled.

ACTIVITY 94

Write the word for the given definition:

1. commonplace = _____

2. second to last = _____

3. extremely awful = _____

4. so-so in quality = _____

5. first in importance = _____

6. unrivaled = _____

Words from Science

Words from science often have a second meaning that is useful to know.

catalyst *(n.)* katl-ist
Something that speeds up the rate of change.

*By not giving up her bus seat, Rosa Parks was a **catalyst** for the Civil Rights movement.*

From the Greek word meaning "to dissolve." As with *fulcrum* and *entropy* (see below) this word has a broader, figurative meaning, referring to anything that brings about something else (see sentence above).

fulcrum *(n.)* fŏŏlkrəm
Something that supplies leverage for action.

*Constant reading is the **fulcrum** of a strong vocabulary.*

This comes from the Latin meaning "to prop up." More broadly speaking, this word can refer to anything that plays an essential role or part in something else.

entropy *(n.)* entrəpē
Disorganization, randomness.

*The school year had an **entropic** quality for Sarah; though organized and predictable at the beginning, it became increasingly chaotic and unmanageable toward the end.*

From the Greek for "transformation." This word, broadly speaking, refers to a disorder or the lack of predictability.

hypothesize *(v.)*
hī'päθə͵sīz
To come up with an initial theory or explanation for something.

empirical *(adj.)* em'pirikəl
Based on what the senses can perceive.

centripetal *(adj.)*
sen'tripətl
Moving away from a center point.

irrefutable *(adj.)*
irə'fyōotəbəl
Unable to be disproven.

ACTIVITY 95

Write the word for the given definition:

1. unable to be disproven = _____

2. based on what the senses can perceive = _____

3. moving away from a center point = _____

4. something that supplies leverage for action = _____

5. to come up with an initial theory = _____

6. something that speeds up the rate of change = _____

Is It Everywhere or Anywhere?

Some of these words describe the omnipresent, while others depict the opposite.

pervasive *(adj.)* pərˈvāsiv
Describing something negative that is common throughout an area.

*Texting while driving has become increasingly **pervasive**.*

From the Latin for "to spread through." A similar word is *prevalent*.

ubiquitous *(adj.)* yo͞oˈbikwətəs
Appearing everywhere.

*The sight of somebody wearing headphones while walking down the street has become a **ubiquitous** feature of urban life.*

This comes from the Latin meaning "everywhere." The noun form of this word is *ubiquity*.

ascendant *(adj.)* əˈsendənt
Gaining influence.

*Many once-obscure figures are **ascendant** on YouTube, attracting millions of new fans each month.*

From the Latin for "climbing up."

predominate *(v.)*
priˈdäməˌnāt
To be greatest in number or extent.

sparse *(adj.)* spärs
Not populated, scattered.

rampant *(adj.)* rampənt
Describing something negative that is found everywhere.

rife *(adj.)* rīf
Describing something harmful or negative that is widespread.

diminish *(v.)* diˈminiSH
To become less.

ACTIVITY 96

Mark "S" if the meanings of the two words are similar, "O" if they are opposite, or "D" if they are different:

1. rife and diminish _____

2. predominate and ascendant _____

3. sparse and pervasive _____

4. ubiquitous and rampant _____

Thou Doth Complain Too Much

These words describe different levels of expressing dissatisfaction, whether one is begging for something to be done or simply complaining.

petulant *(adj.)* peCHələnt
Moody, whiny.

When his wishes were not immediately satisfied, the lead actor became petulant.

From the Latin for "impudent," which means "rude." A synonym for *petulant*, and one common on some standardized tests, is *querulous*.

peevish *(adj.)* pēviSH
Easily upset by trivial things.

It was hard to go on a road trip with her because she was peevish, every few minutes finding something else to gripe about.

This word comes from Middle English for "foolish" and "insane." This word is related to the noun *peeve*, as in "pet peeve," which is a specific dislike somebody has.

entreat *(v.)* enˈtrēt
To plead.

She entreated the guards to let her see her son.

From the Latin word for "to handle." *Beseech* and *implore* are two good synonyms to know.

supplicate *(v.)*
səpliˌkāt
To beg for something earnestly.

remonstrate *(v.)*
riˈmänˌstrāt
To protest loudly.

gainsay *(v.)* gānˈsā
To deny a statement or to challenge someone.

adjure *(v.)* əˈjo͞or
To earnestly ask or urge somebody.

ACTIVITY 97

Mark "S" if the meanings of the two words are similar, "O" if they are opposite, or "D" if they are different:

1. adjure and remonstrate _____

2. gainsay and supplicate _____

3. beseech and implore _____

4. entreat and peevish _____

Nothing Is Going to Stop Us Now . . . or Is It?

These words either energize us or hold us back.

thwart *(v.)* θwôrt
To prevent someone or something from achieving a goal.

*The rain **thwarted** their attempt to reach the mountain peak before nightfall.*

From a Middle English word meaning "difficult to manage." A good synonym is *frustrate*.

galvanize *(v.)* galvə͵nīz
To stimulate or excite into action.

*The rescue team was **galvanized** when two injured people were pulled from the wreckage, and they began working with renewed intensity.*

This word is taken from the name of Luigi Galvani, an Italian scientist who used electric current to make the limbs of dead frogs move. *Spur* and *rouse* are two verbs with similar meanings.

stymie *(v.)* stīmē
To block one's progress.

*A lack of funds and volunteers **stymied** the effort to clean up the city center.*

The only word in this book that has its origins in the game of golf, a *stymie* occurs when an opponent's ball blocks the hole. This word is typically used informally.

inexorable *(adj.)*
inˈeksərəbəl
Incapable of being stopped.

tonic *(n.)* tänik
Something that invigorates or endows with sudden life and energy.

indomitable *(adj.)*
inˈdämitəbəl
Impossible to stop or defeat.

ACTIVITY 98

Mark "S" if the meanings of the two words are similar, "O" if they are opposite, or "D" if they are different:

1. stymie and galvanize _____

2. thwart and inexorable _____

3. indomitable and tonic _____

Spoils of War

War has given us an extensive arsenal of vocabulary.

armistice (n.) ärməstəs
An agreement between two warring sides to stop fighting.

After both countries had lost tens of thousands of soldiers, an **armistice** *was reached.*

From the French for "arms stoppage." *Truce* and *cease-fire* are common synonyms.

entente (n.) änˈtänt
An alliance between groups based on a friendly understanding.

There is an **entente** *between many prosperous nations today not to wage war against the other.*

This word comes from the French for "friendly understanding." The Entente Cordiale was a 1904 agreement between England and France to provide one another with assistance during wartime if necessary. This agreement proved significant during World War I.

cede (v.) sēd
To give up or surrender.

Since the early 1990s, rock music has **ceded** *ground to hip-hop music, which has remained the dominant genre throughout the 2000s.*

From the French for "to yield." When describing territory, *cede* is an antonym of *annex*.

accord (n.) əˈkôrd
Harmonious relations between groups or countries.

annex (v.) əˈneks
To acquire or add territory, typically when a more powerful country seizes land from a less powerful country.

maraud (v.) məˈrôd
To raid and pillage.

martial (adj.) märSHəl
Relating to war.

revanchism (n.) rəˈvänSHizəm
The seeking of lost territory.

ACTIVITY 99

Write the word that completes the sentence:

1. Genghis Khan and his followers were known for _____ villages.

2. The size of the country did not change much during the war, because though it was able to _____ some territory, it also had to _____ some to the enemy.

3. The two nations are marked by an _____ that has led to decades of peace.

4. The _____ was short-lived, and fighting soon broke out again.

5. The two nations had an _____, so that if either were attacked by another country, the other would intercede.

Are You Likeable?

Whether you are friendly or grouchy or somewhere in between, there is a word to describe you.

cordial *(adj.)* kôrjəl
Polite and warm, eager to accommodate.

He was always given a **cordial** *reception at the Stewarts' home—until they found out he'd been spreading rumors about them.*

From the Latin for "heart." The noun *cordial* is another term for *liqueur*.

aloof *(adj.)* əˈlo͞of
Distant, standoffish.

Val, the only single person among the large group of couples, chose to remain **aloof***.*

This word has a nautical origin and describes a boat moving away from the shore and into the wind. It's important to remember that the word *aloof* typically contains the element of distance. So if somebody is standing next to you, not engaging with you, aloof might not be the best word. But if a person is standing on the other side of the room from everybody else, looking away with their arms crossed, aloof is a good word.

misanthrope *(n.)* misən‚θrōp
A person who hates other people and shuns their company.

He might have seemed a **misanthrope** *in public—always scowling when others tried smiling at him—but at home he was a doting father.*

From the Greek for "to hate man."

congenial *(adj.)* kənˈjēnyəl
Friendly and pleasant to be around.

amiable *(adj.)* āmēəbəl
Friendly and pleasant.

abominable *(adj.)* əˈbäm(ə)nəbəl
Despicable and loathsome.

odious *(adj.)* ōdēəs
Worthy of hate.

curmudgeon *(n.)* kərˈməjən
A grouchy, ill-tempered person.

ACTIVITY 100

Match the word with its definition:

1. worthy of hate _____

2. a grouchy person _____

3. despicable _____

4. a person who hates other people _____

5. polite and warm _____

6. distant, standoffish _____

a. misanthrope

b. cordial

c. odious

d. abominable

e. aloof

f. curmudgeon

Hurtful Words

English is full of words that mean "to harshly insult" or "to slander."

lambaste *(v.)* lamˈbāst
To criticize harshly.

*The coach **lambasted** the team for blowing a comfortable lead in the final quarter.*

From an Old English word meaning "to beat."

acrimonious *(adj.)* akrəˈmōnēəs
Describing relations or speech marked by extreme bitterness.

*What had begun as an earnest debate became so **acrimonious** that both sides were soon hurling insults.*

From the Latin for "bitter." The related word *acrid* is commonly used to describe taste or smell, though it can also be used in a similar sense as *acrimonious*.

excoriate *(v.)* ikˈskôrēˌāt
To criticize extremely harshly.

*Once it was revealed that the mayor had accepted bribes from an organized crime syndicate, he was **excoriated** in the press.*

This comes from the Latin "to tear the skin off of." *Excoriate* can still be used to mean "to tear off the flesh," though this usage is less common.

invidious *(adj.)* inˈvidēəs
Causing resentment or envy.

aspersion *(n.)* əˈspərZHən
A verbal attack on a person's character.

rail *(v.)* rāl
To speak out harshly and at length against.

inveigh *(v.)* inˈvā
To complain, protest against.

vituperative *(adj.)*
vəˈt(y)o͞opəˌrātiv
Describing words that are extremely harsh.

ACTIVITY 101

Fill in the missing letters to complete the word:

1. l___b___te

2. _ai_

3. __per___on

4. __vid___s

5. ___tup___ive

6. in___gh

How Pure?

The meanings behind these words range from pure to impure.

immaculate *(adj.)* iˈmakyələt
Perfect, free from any blemish.

*His resume was **immaculate**, except for the one year that he was unemployed.*

From the Latin for "stained." The *im-* negates this. A good synonym to know is *pristine*.

defile *(v.)* diˈfīl
To ruin something that is considered sacred.

*The bandits **defiled** the city's sacred temple, spray-painting it red.*

From the Old French for "to trample upon." This word can also mean "to impair the quality of something."

adulterate *(v.)* əˈdəltəˌrāt
To mix with something inferior, thereby tainting the original.

*In order to save money, the restaurant **adulterated** the freshly squeezed orange juice with frozen concentrate.*

This comes from the Latin for "corrupted." *Unadulterated* means "pure, not mixed with anything bad."

degrade *(v.)* diˈgrād
To lower the quality of something.

sully *(v.)* səlē
To damage the reputation, blemish, stain.

unblemished *(adj.)*
ənˈblemiSHt
Without any stain, perfect.

vitiate *(v.)* viSHēˌāt
To corrupt or ruin the quality.

ACTIVITY 102

Mark "S" if the meanings of the two words are similar, "O" if they are opposite, or "D" if they are different:

1. degrade and sully _____

2. unblemished and vitiated _____

3. adulterated and immaculate _____

How Do I Express Myself?

English has many words that describe sayings or expressions.

dictum *(n.)* diktəm
A general expression or saying.

*A **dictum** among the gym goers was "no pain, no gain"—until one of them tore a muscle.*

From the Latin for "thing said." A *dictum* can also be an official declaration.

platitude *(n.)* plati͵t(y)o͞od
A trite remark that offers no value but is often said in earnest.

*His aunt offered many **platitudes**, but the one she most often uttered was "everything happens for a reason."*

This word comes from the French for "flat." *Platitude* is one of the longest words in English in which removing the first letter results in a word with a totally unrelated meaning (*platitude* → *latitude*).

aphorism *(n.)* afə͵rizəm
A concise saying.

*The self-help guru spoke in **aphorisms**—one day at a time, becoming is part of being—though by the end of his seminars, they sounded more like platitudes.*

From the Greek "to define." A far less common word, but one that might show up on the GRE, is *apothegm*.

cliché *(n.)* klēˈSHā
An idea or expression that lacks originality.

maxim *(n.)* maksim
A short saying.

precept *(n.)* prēˌsept
A general principle or rule.

bromide *(n.)* brōmīd
A platitude.

ACTIVITY 103

Provide the word for the given definition:

1. a short saying (2 possible answers) = _____

2. a general expression = _____

3. a general principle or rule = _____

4. an overused, unoriginal saying (3 possible answers) = _____

Getting Better or Getting Worse?

The words below can explain both the lessening and the intensifying of bad things.

abate (*v.*) əˈbāt
To lessen, as something negative or undesirable.

*The winds that had whipped up the forest fire finally **abated**.*

This comes from the Latin "to beat." *Abate* is the opposite of the next word, *exacerbate*.

exacerbate (*v.*) igˈzasərˌbāt
To make something bad worse.

*The jackhammer outside her window **exacerbated** her headache.*

This comes from Latin and shares a similar root as *acerbic*, which means "bitter." *Exacerbate* should not be confused with *exasperate*, which means "to annoy."

truncate (*v.*) trəNGˌkāt
To shorten by cutting off the end.

*The teacher's passionate discussion about the French Revolution was **truncated** by the class bell.*

From the Latin for "maimed." *Curtail* is a good synonym to know.

escalate (*v.*) eskəˌlāt
To increase in number or extent.

curtail (*v.*) kərˈtāl
To reduce in number or extent.

assuage (*v.*) əˈswāj
To make something less bad, soothe.

augment (*v.*) ôgˈment
To increase.

cessation (*n.*) seˈsāSHən
An end or interruption.

ACTIVITY 104

Write the word that completes each sentence:

1. Her hostile words will only _____ the situation, and everybody will start arguing. (2 possible answers)

2. At first it was difficult to _____ his anger, but eventually he calmed down.

3. By surrendering the most northerly part of its territory, the nation was effectively _____.

4. The storm _____ by morning time, though significant damage had already been done.

5. With a _____ of hostilities on the horizon, the two nations looked ahead to a time of healing.

It's All About the Self

These words are literally built around the "self"—though some are the exact opposite of *selfish*.

self-aggrandizing *(adj.)* ˌself əˈɡranˌdīziNG
Portraying oneself as highly important.

Though his accomplishments were modest at best, the **self-aggrandizing** *senator frequently dropped comments that he would run for president.*

This comes from the Latin for "large." *Aggrandize* is also a word, though it is not nearly as common as *self-aggrandize* or *self-aggrandizing*.

self-deprecating *(adj.)* self ˈdeprəˌkādiNG
Putting oneself down in a humorous and playful way so as to come across as modest.

The concert pianist was **self-deprecating** *about her virtuosity, telling others that anyone who'd practiced as much as she did was bound to be pretty decent.*

From the Latin for "to pray against oneself." *Self-depreciating* is a synonym and very similar-looking word, though it is far less common.

altruistic *(adj.)* altro͞oˈistik
Putting others before oneself.

The career of a firefighter is one of the most **altruistic** *occupations, because every day these men and women risk their lives to save complete strangers.*

This is from the Italian for "somebody else."

modest *(adj.)* mädəst
Not bringing attention to oneself or one's accomplishments.

selfless *(adj.)* selfləs
Putting others' needs before one's own.

egotistical *(adj.)* ēɡəˈtistək(ə)l
Attaching great importance to oneself and constantly talking about oneself.

self-effacing *(adj.)* self əˈfāsiNG
Focusing attention away from oneself.

self-abnegation *(n.)* self abnəˈɡāSH(ə)n
The total denial of oneself or bringing oneself down to a lower level.

ACTIVITY 105

Write the word that completes each sentence:

1. Mother Theresa was known for being _____, always putting aside any selfish desires and offering up her life in service of the poor. (2 possible answers)

2. The author was so _____ that he went into hiding whenever a book of his was about to be published.

3. Despite his remarkable talents on the lute, he was _____ about his extraordinary performance, chalking it up to lots of practice.

4. He was known for his _____ wit, always poking fun at himself.

5. Chester has not amounted to much, though he is terribly _____, as you can tell by looking at all the photos on his social media homepage.

Three-Letter Words

Three-letter words are often overlooked on account of their diminutive stature, but they can really pack a punch.

eke *(v.)* ēk
To supplement or make last, to obtain in small quantity.

*The couple was forced to **eke** out their existence in a local shelter, asking strangers for spare change.*

This comes from Old English meaning "to increase." This word is also used in sports, in cases where one team barely beats out the other, as in *eke out an overtime win.*

mar *(v.)* mär
To damage the appearance or quality.

*She wanted to **mar** her rival's reputation by creating a constant swirl of online rumors.*

From an Old English word meaning "to damage." *Unmarred*, meaning "unblemished" or "untainted," is also a relatively common word.

imp *(n.)* imp
A naughty, misbehaving child.

*When the little boy went without a nap, he became an **imp**, throwing plates and glasses on the floor while cackling malevolently.*

In Old English, this word referred to the child of a devil. *Impish* is the adjective form of the word.

ire *(n.)* ī(ə)r
Anger.

vie *(v.)* vī
To compete.

woe *(n.)* wō
Pain and anguish.

nub *(n.)* nəb
The central point of an issue.

ACTIVITY 106

Provide the word for the given definition:

1. pain and anguish = _____

2. to compete = _____

3. a naughty child = _____

4. to damage the appearance or quality of = _____

5. to supplement or make last = _____

6. anger = _____

7. the central point of an issue = _____

Four-Letter Words

Four-letter words are also commonly neglected.

char *(v.)* CHär
To burn something just enough so that its surface turns black.

*Many prefer their meat a little **charred**, as long as the inside is still slightly pink.*

This word comes from *charcoal*. This is a word that likely becomes quite popular during the Fourth of July weekend.

pith *(n.)* piθ
The essence of something.

*The **pith** of agnosticism is that, ultimately, there is no way of determining whether a higher being truly exists.*

Comes from Old English. The *pith* can also describe the inner rind of citrus fruits.

carp *(v.)* kärp
To complain constantly over trivial matters.

*He **carped** at his colleagues, pointing out every small mistake they made.*

This term comes from the Latin for "to slander." A *carp* is also a freshwater fish.

moil *(v.)* moil
To toil away.

foil *(v.)* foil
To prevent someone (typically bad) from achieving a goal.

curt *(adj.)* kərt
Rude and abrupt, brusque.

deft *(adj.)* deft
Skillful.

crux *(n.)* krəks
The most important or central point.

ACTIVITY 107

Provide the word for the given definition:

1. to toil away = _____

2. to prevent someone from achieving a goal = _____

3. the essence of something = _____

4. rude, brusque = _____

5. skillful = _____

6. the most important point = _____

7. to complain constantly = _____

8. to burn something just enough so that its surface turns black = _____

Very Long Words

These words are certainly memorable for their size—but often difficult to remember.

indefatigable *(adj.)* indəˈfatigəbəl
Not giving up or tiring, unwavering.

In his fight for Indian independence, Mahatma Gandhi was **indefatigable**—*no amount of physical hardship or bullying could deter him from achieving this goal.*

Originally from a Latin word meaning "cannot be wearied." This word could have also made the commonly confused word list because the *in-* and the *de-* suggest a double negative, implying that this word is synonymous with *fatigue*.

infinitesimal *(adj.)* infiniˈtes(ə)məl
Extremely small.

To the unaided eye, the distance between some stars seems **infinitesimal**, *though they may in fact be many light-years away.*

This is from a Modern Latin word meaning "infinitely small." Yet another word that is commonly confused (and very long!), *infinitesimal* does not relate to infinity but the very opposite: something extremely minute.

commensurate *(adj.)* kəˈmensərət
In proportion or relation to.

The legal system is predicated on the idea that a sentence should be **commensurate** *with the crime, with murder charges often bringing the harshest punishment.*

From the Latin for "to measure with." This word is typically used in formal contexts.

disenchantment *(n.)*
disenˈCHantmənt
The process by which one is stripped of one's illusions.

prognostication *(n.)*
prägˌnästəˈkāSHən
A prediction or prophecy.

indemnification *(n.)*
inˈdemnəfiˈkāSHən
Protection from being sued or having legal responsibility in a matter.

unprepossessing *(adj.)*
ənˌprēpəˈzesiNG
Unattractive.

pulchritudinous *(adj.)*
pəlkrəˌt(y)ōōdənəs
Beautiful.

ACTIVITY 108

Write the word that completes each sentence:

1. His _____ that his son's Little League team would win seemed farfetched, but in the end, they upset the best team in town.

2. His _____ with the world of politics drove him to become a schoolteacher.

3. Is success a result of talent or is it _____ with the amount of time and passion we invest?

4. Far from an _____ voice in the school's attempt to avoid a strike, he quickly backed down when his own job was at stake.

5. The differences between the designs of the two computers is _____, so it won't be surprising if a lawsuit is in the offing.

Can You Feel It?

These words describe relative states of density and tangibility, from solid to ethereal.

cumbersome *(adj.)* kəmbərsəm
Difficult or awkward to carry because it is heavy.

*While many imagine knights to be efficient killers, one cannot help but think that with all their **cumbersome** armor, knights moved very laboriously.*

This comes from the archaic verb *cumber*, which means "to hinder" or "to obstruct." *Unwieldy* is a good synonym.

palpable *(adj.)* palpəbəl
Able to be touched, tangible.

*The excitement was **palpable** minutes before the diva took the stage.*

From the Latin for "to touch gently." *Palpable* is typically used to describe an atmosphere or an emotion so intense that it's as though one can feel it, whereas *tangible* describes something that can actually be touched.

gossamer *(n.)* gäsəmər
Something very light and delicate.

*To the unaided eye, the millipede's many legs were **gossamer**.*

Likely from "goose summer," a time in late November when geese are eaten. Another definition of *gossamer* describes the fine, filmy substance out of which small spiders spin cobwebs.

indiscernible *(adj.)*
indəˈsərnəb(ə)l
Unable to be seen.

insubstantial *(adj.)*
insəbˈstan(t)SH(ə)l
Light and delicate, not having solid form or strength.

intangible *(adj.)*
inˈtanjəb(ə)l
Unable to be touched, abstract.

translucent *(adj.)*
transˈlo͞osnt
Somewhat transparent so that light can shine through.

ACTIVITY 109

Mark "S" if the meanings of the two words are similar, "O" if they are opposite, or "D" if they are different:

1. translucent and intangible _____

2. insubstantial and gossamer _____

3. impalpable and cumbersome _____

4. indiscernible and palpable _____

What's All the Fuss?

Some of these words illustrate conflict, whereas others describe the easing of such hostility.

fracas (*n.*) frākəs
A loud commotion or argument.

*The **fracas** in the hallway between two feuding neighbors woke him up at one in the morning.*

From the Italian for "making an uproar." *Melee* is a similar word, but it suggests more of an actual fight or scuffle, usually involving a group of people.

furor (*n.*) fyo͞or͵ôr
A public outcry over something shameful.

*The **furor** over the Watergate political scandal led to the president resigning.*

This comes from the Latin for "rage." The British spelling of this word is *furore* (in case you happen to be reading any British writers).

détente (*n.*) dā'tänt
The lessening of hostility between nations.

*The **détente** between the two tech behemoths is likely the result of both having lost so much to each other in costly litigation.*

From the French for "relaxation." This word should not be confused with *entente*, a mutual understanding between nations regarding their political relations.

hullabaloo (*n.*)
ˈhələbə͵lo͞o
A big uproar or fuss.

ado (*n.*) əˈdo͞o
A fuss.

fiasco (*n.*) fēˈaskō
Something that ends up a complete failure.

reconciliation (*n.*)
rekən͵silēˈāSHən
The restoring of harmonious relations.

rift (*n.*) rift
A sudden and often irreparable break in a relationship.

ACTIVITY 110

Provide the word with the given origin:

1. from the Italian for "uproar" = _____

2. from the Latin for "rage" = _____

3. from the French for "relaxation" = _____

Unscramble the word:

4. doa _____

5. firt _____

6. eleme _____

7. cofias _____

What's the Bright Idea? (PART 1)

Some ideas are original, whereas others can be described by the words below.

derivative *(adj.)* diˈrivətiv
Taken from another source, not original.

*The singer's style is totally **derivative**, taking from every 1980s pop song he can think of.*

This word comes from the Latin for "downstream." This word usually refers to ideas or creative products, especially art and music.

orthodox *(adj.)* ôrTHəˌdäks
Following or conforming to what is accepted as the standard.

*Since he didn't like offending anyone, he always expressed the **orthodox** views on most subjects.*

From the Latin *ortho-* for "straight" (as in *orthodontist*, a teeth straightener) and *dox-* meaning "opinion."

pedestrian *(adj.)* pəˈdestrēən
Lacking imagination or originality.

*Until they won the lottery and traveled the world, they had led **pedestrian** lives.*

From the Latin for "going on foot" (giving us the common definition) and also from the Latin for "resembling prose" (giving us the less common definition explained here). This word is similar to *prosaic* in two ways: It is a synonym and is also derived from the word *prose*.

banal *(adj.)* bəˈnäl, bəˈnal
Lacking originality.

hackneyed *(adj.)* haknēd
Lacking originality.

trite *(adj.)* trīt
Lacking originality.

prosaic *(adj.)* prəˈzāik
Lacking beauty.

quotidian *(adj.)*
kwōˈtidēən
Occurring daily, commonplace.

ACTIVITY 111

Fill in the missing letters to complete the word and give the definition:

1. _rit_ _____

2. ha____yed _____

3. ___sai_ _____

4. b_n_l _____

5. __otid__n _____

6. ___estria_ _____

What's the Bright Idea? (PART 2)

These words are all about originality.

pioneering *(adj.)* pīəˈniriNG
Using new ways or methods.

*Her **pioneering** research into the extinction of the lowland gorilla influenced how many subsequent studies were conducted in the wild.*

From the French for "foot soldier." A good way to remember *pioneering* is to think of the pioneers, or the *first* Europeans to enter upon new land in the Americas.

avant-garde *(n.)* avänt ̍gärd
Those who create the newest ideas, typically in the arts.

*He was part of the **avant-garde** whose art form consisted of walking through canvasses thereby destroying them.*

From the French for "vanguard" or "the head of an army." The *avant-garde* is typically known for outlandish ideas and is used to describe many trends in twentieth-century art and music.

maverick *(n.)* mav(ə)rik
A person known for having unorthodox views.

*Einstein was a bit of a **maverick**, thinking about the dimensions of time and space, while his contemporaries remained fixated on atomic structure.*

This word comes from Samuel Maverick, a Texas rancher (yes, some words are derived from America!) who was known for not branding his cattle. Famous business mavericks of the last few decades include Steve Jobs, Richard Branson, and Jeff Bezos.

visionary *(n.)* viZHə ̱nerē
One known for having pioneering ideas.

unconventional *(n.)* ənkənˈven(t)SH(ə)n(ə)l
Not typical or ordinary.

radical *(n.)* radək(ə)l
Someone with extreme views, often of a political nature.

ACTIVITY 112

Mark "T" for true and "F" for false:

1. a maverick is known for having orthodox views _____

2. someone who is a radical is unlikely to rebel _____

3. one starting a new business is likely to be a visionary _____

4. the avant-garde of the art world can be described as conservative _____

5. someone who is pioneering is likely to think outside of the box _____

Get Off the Couch!

Whether through flattery or threat, these words describe the act of influencing.

nudge *(v.)* nəj
To encourage someone in a gentle manner.

*His parents had always **nudged** him to get better grades, but when he came home with mostly C's, they became far less patient.*

From the Norwegian meaning "to push." "To lightly prod" is another good way of thinking of this word.

coerce *(v.)* kōˈərs
To persuade someone to do something by using threats.

*By threatening to take away his video game system, she **coerced** her brother into divulging where he'd hidden the candy.*

From the Latin for "to restrain together." The noun form of this word is *coercion*.

duress *(n.)* d(y)o͞oˈres
Forcible restraint, compulsion by threat.

*He was under **duress** when he revealed his password to the thieves.*

This comes from the Latin for "hard." Unlike *coercion*, which takes the verb form *coerce*, *duress* does not have a corresponding verb.

coax *(v.)* kōks
To use flattery to get someone to do something.

goad *(v.)* gōd
To provoke someone to get them to do something.

induce *(v.)* inˈd(y)o͞os
To persuade someone to do something.

cajole *(v.)* kəˈjōl
To persistently coax and flatter someone to get them to do something.

blandishment *(n.)*
blandiSHmənt
Flattery of someone toward getting them to do something.

ACTIVITY 113

Mark "S" if the meanings of the two words are similar, "O" if they are opposite, or "D" if they are different (in terms of methods used):

1. duress and blandishment _____

2. induce and cajole _____

3. nudge and coerce _____

4. goad and coax _____

Is This Confusing?

Hopefully these words about confusion don't bewilder you, and you can maintain your clarity.

perplexed *(adj.)* pərˈplekst
To be completely confused.

*The American tourists were utterly **perplexed** walking around downtown Tokyo, where no signs were written in English.*

From the Latin for "entangled." *Perplexed* is not quite as extreme as *baffled*, which is less extreme than *dumbfounded*.

equanimity *(n.)* ēkwəˈnimitē
Calmness and composure.

*Even in the worst of traffic jams, she exuded **equanimity**, courtesy of the classical-music radio station.*

This comes from the Latin for "equal mind." *Imperturbability* is a synonym.

imperturbable *(adj.)* impərˈtərbəbəl
Not easily disturbed or upset, calm.

*Despite the jets roaring in the sky above, the cows were **imperturbable**, chewing on their cud.*

Comes from the Latin for "not disturbed." *Self-possessed* and *coolheaded* are two common synonyms of *imperturbable*.

poised *(adj.)* poizd
Confidently composed, not likely to lose one's cool.

flummox *(v.)* fləməks
To perplex.

discombobulated *(adj.)* diskəmˈbäbyəlātəd
Totally confused.

aplomb *(n.)* əˈpläm
Poise and self-assurance.

baffle *(v.)* bafəl
To completely perplex.

ACTIVITY 114

Mark "S" if the meanings of the two words are similar, "O" if they are opposite, or "D" if they are different:

1. baffled and flummoxed _____

2. poise and aplomb _____

3. discombobulated and imperturbable _____

4. equanimity and poise _____

Anyone's Guess

Though we frequently speak with conviction, we might lack strong evidence.

speculation *(n.)* spekyəˈlāSHən
A theory made without strong evidence.

*Till now, the existence of aliens has been pure **speculation**.*

From the Latin for "watchtower." *Speculate* is the verb and *speculative* is the adjective.

conjecture *(n.)* kənˈjekCHər
A guess based on little evidence or information.

*Whether there is a ninth planet in our solar system, hidden in total darkness, remains a matter of **conjecture**.*

This word is from the Latin for "a group of facts." *Conjecture* can also be a verb, synonymous with *surmise*.

presumption *(n.)* priˈzəmpSHən
Acceptance of something as true.

*A **presumption** of guilt is what prosecutors use to build their cases, trying to point out any inconsistency in the defendant's testimony that would point to wrongdoing.*

Another word from Latin, this time meaning "anticipation." The adjective *presumptuous* describes behavior that is overly familiar and even inappropriate, as in: *He sat down next to his new boss, slapped him on the back presumptuously, and said, "Hey, buddy."*

aver *(v.)* əˈvər
To state something emphatically.

submit *(v.)* səbˈmit
To offer up as a theory.

postulate *(v.)*
päsCHəˌlāt
To come up with a hypothesis or theory.

posit *(v.)* päzit
To claim.

ACTIVITY 115

Write the word that completes each sentence:

1. He made a _____ and invited himself to his friend's birthday.

2. It was pure _____, according to the judge, because no evidence had been offered up. (2 possible answers)

Unscramble the word:

3. misbut _____

4. spoit _____

5. rave _____

6. osuppermint _____

Harmful or Harmless?

Some of these words mean "harmful" or "destructive," while others imply quite the opposite. Can you guess, just by looking at them, which is which?

innocuous *(adj.)* iˈnäkyo͞oəs
Not harmful.

*He thought his comment was **innocuous**, but she took offense.*

This comes from the Latin for "not injurious." *Nocuous*, meaning "harmful," is the opposite of *innocuous*, though this word is not very common.

insidious *(adj.)* inˈsidēəs
Harmful in a subtle way.

*Tooth decay is **insidious** because unless your dentist points it out to you, you can't see it.*

From the Latin for "cunning" or "lying in wait for." *Pernicious* is a synonym of *insidious*.

salubrious *(adj.)* səˈlo͞obrēəs
Promoting health.

*The mountain air was **salubrious** for the couple accustomed to the constant auto fumes of urban living.*

Comes from the Latin for "health." *Insalubrious*—meaning "unhealthy"—is also a word, though not nearly as common.

revitalize *(v.)* rēˈvītlˌīz
To bring new life to or inject with life.

pernicious *(adj.)*
pərˈniSHəs
Subtly destructive.

restorative *(adj.)*
riˈstôrətiv
Providing energy.

deleterious *(adj.)*
deliˈti(ə)rēəs
Harmful, destructive.

ACTIVITY 116

Mark "S" if the meanings of the two words are similar, "O" if they are opposite, or "D" if they are different:

1. salubrious and pernicious _____

2. restorative and salubrious _____

3. insidious and restorative _____

4. deleterious and innocuous _____

The Anger Meter

Just as one can measure different degrees of happiness, anger comes in many shapes and sizes.

indignant *(adj.)* inˈdignənt
Angry over perceived injustice.

When people cut in line, others behind them feel **indignant** *at their brazen attitude.*

From the Latin for "deeming unworthy." This word is similar to *resentful*, though that term has a tinge of bitterness to it.

bristle *(v.)* brisəl
To react angrily, typically by standing more erect and with the chest out.

When his friends criticized his bad driving, he **bristled***, straightening his shoulders and frowning.*

This word comes from Old English. A bristle can also be a short, stiff hair.

disgruntled *(adj.)* disˈgrən(t)ld
Aggrieved, dissatisfied.

He'd worked 80 hours a week for a year without getting a raise, so he became understandingly **disgruntled** *when his boss asked him to take on even more.*

From a word meaning "little grunts." A common synonym is *dissatisfied* and a not-quite-as-common synonym is *disaffected*.

incensed *(adj.)* inˈsenst
Enraged.

peeve *(v.)* pēv
To annoy, irk.

piqued *(adj.)* pēkt
Irritated.

irate *(adj.)* īˈrāt
Furious.

wrath *(n.)* raθ
Extreme anger.

ACTIVITY 117

Write the word that completes each sentence:

1. The coach's _____ was legendary: He had thrown no fewer than 12 water coolers during close losses.

2. When she found out that she was not invited to the party, she was _____ but not really that mad; a few days later, she was over it. (2 possible answers)

3. The man was _____ that once again his family had left all their dirty dishes in the sink for him to wash. (2 possible answers)

4. He was _____, complaining to his friends that once again he'd been passed over for a promotion.

From Cowardly to Courageous

There are many words for the levels of courage and fear, from timid to intimidating.

intrepid *(adj.)* inˈtrepid
Fearless.

*The **intrepid** explorers ventured deep into Antarctica, where none had ventured before.*

From the Latin for "not alarmed." The noun *trepidation* means "fear."

formidable *(adj.)* fôrmədəbəl
Intimidating, arousing fear.

*The high school football team was state champion, a **formidable** opponent to all the other schools in its district.*

This comes from the Latin for "fear." This word can also describe a person's mind or intellect.

craven *(adj.)* krāvən
Cowardly and despicable.

*Street cameras have caught people committing such **craven** crimes as stripping jewelry from pedestrians who had been hit by vehicles.*

From the French for "crushed" or "overwhelmed." *Lily-livered* and *chickenhearted* are two more informal synonyms.

undaunted *(adj.)*
ənˈdôntid
Not intimidated.

plucky *(adj.)* pləkē
Brave in a spirited manner.

valorous *(adj.)* ˈvalərəs
Possessing or acting with bold bravery.

pusillanimous *(adj.)*
pyo͞osəˈlanəməs
Lacking courage.

redoubtable *(adj.)*
riˈdoutəbəl
Formidable.

ACTIVITY 118

Fill in the missing letters to complete each word and give the definition:

1. ___tre___d _____

2. _luck_ _____

3. va___ous _____

4. red___table _____

5. __sill___mous _____

6. _rave_ _____

I Have an Official Announcement to Make

The following words all describe official declarations.

edict *(n.)* ēdikt
A decree or proclamation.

*The government's **edict** set strict curfew laws.*

From the Latin for "to say out." The Edict of Nantes, signed in 1598 by Henry IV, granted tolerance to Protestants, thereby ending the Wars of Religion.

abrogate *(v.)* abrəˌgāt
To cancel or overturn a law (used in formal contexts).

*In 1933, the government **abrogated** Prohibition via the Twenty-First Amendment, thereby ending the thirteen-year period during which it was illegal to sell and/or consume alcohol.*

Comes from the Latin for "to repeal." The word *repeal* is the synonym more commonly used. *Abrogate* should be reserved for more formal contexts, such as an academic or legal paper.

promulgate *(v.)* prämələˌgāt
To declare officially or make widely known.

*The changes to paid time off were **promulgated** throughout the company months before taking effect.*

This comes from the Latin for "to make public." "To publicize officially" is a good way to think of this word.

enact *(v.)* enˈakt
To make into law.

annul *(v.)* əˈnəl
To overturn, declare invalid.

fiat *(n.)* fēət
An official order by a person in a position of power, or a decree.

rescind *(v.)* riˈsind
To revoke, cancel, repeal.

ACTIVITY 119

Mark "S" if the meanings of the two words are the same, "R" if they are related, and "NR" if they are not related:

1. rescind and annul _____

2. enact and promulgate _____

3. abrogate and rescind _____

4. fiat and edict _____

Hold On to Your Wits! From Dull to Sharp

These words describe different levels of insight, judgment, intelligence, and more.

obtuse *(adj.)* əbˈt(y)o͞os
Unintelligent, not able to grasp ideas or concepts easily.

*My father felt terribly **obtuse** when working the television remote, even though I had shown him countless times how to do so.*

From Middle English for "blunt." In geometry, *obtuse* is used to describe angles that are greater than 90 degrees. Acute angles are used to describe angles less than 90 degrees. Interestingly, *acute* is the opposite of *obtuse*, in the sense that it is used in the example sentence; somebody who is *acute* is quick to mentally grasp something.

niche *(n.)* niCH, nēSH
One's special area of expertise.

*His **niche** was go-kart racing, and he had at one point taken part in a national competition.*

From the French for "to make a nest." A *niche* can also be a little hole or cavity in a wall where you can store things.

astute *(adj.)* əˈst(y)o͞ot
Having a sharp intelligence that allows one to get a quick grasp of situations.

*She was highly **astute** and was not fooled by the credit card scam as many others had been.*

From the Latin for "craft." This word is a synonym with *shrewd*.

acumen *(n.)* əˈkyo͞omən
Good judgment in a specific context.

shrewd *(adj.)* shro͞od
Having keen judgment.

acute *(adj.)* əˈkyo͞ot
Extremely sharp and insightful.

bailiwick *(n.)* bāləˌwik
One's area of learning or knowledge.

ACTIVITY 120

Provide the word for the given definition:

1. having sharp, keen judgment (3 possible answers) = _____

2. not able to grasp ideas or concepts easily = _____

3. a special area of learning or knowledge (2 possible answers) = _____

Prefix: *Ben-*

These words are all built upon the Latin root *ben-*,
meaning "good."

benign *(adj.)* biˈnīn
Not harmful, kind.

*The effect on the surrounding area was relatively **benign** considering
some of the dangerous chemicals released.*

This is from the Latin for "well born." This word can also be used
in a medical context when describing a tumor that is not cancerous. The opposite (a cancerous tumor) is described as *malignant*.

benefactor *(n.)* benəˌfaktər
A person who gives money or a gift to another.

*Without her **benefactor**, a former scientist impressed with her skills,
Shelly would not likely have had enough money to attend grad school.*

Again, this is from Latin, meaning "do well." *Patron* is a
similar word.

benediction *(n.)* beniˈdikSHən
A blessing.

*The new converts traveled thousands of miles to hear the **benediction**
of their religious leader.*

This is from the Latin for *ben-* meaning "good" and *dict-* meaning
"to say." This word was traditionally used to refer to Catholicism
but can be extended even to a nonreligious context.

beneficial *(adj.)*
benəˈfiSHəl
Helpful, advantageous.

benevolence *(n.)*
bəˈnevələn(t)s
Kindness.

beneficiary *(n.)*
benəˈfiSHēˌerē
A person who receives
something advantageous.

ACTIVITY 121

Provide the word for the given definition:

1. kind (give 2 words) = _____ _____

2. a noncancerous tumor = _____

3. a person who receives something advantageous = _____

4. a blessing = _____

5. advantageous = _____

Prefix: *Mal-*

In contrast, these words make use of the root *mal-*, meaning "bad."

malaria *(n.)* məˈle(ə)rēə
A disease carried by mosquitos.

Malaria is endemic in many parts of Africa.

Comes from the Italian for "bad air." Other mosquito-borne illnesses include dengue fever and West Nile virus.

malfeasance *(n.)* malˈfēzəns
Wrongdoing, particularly by an official.

Corporate malfeasance is on the rise as recent accounting fraud reveals.

From the French for "wrongdoing."

malapropism *(n.)* maləˌpräpizm
An unintended—usually humorous—misuse of a word or words.

He was notorious for his malapropism, once claiming he hated "oven guard" (not avant-garde) art, especially because the art had nothing to do with ovens.

This word comes from a character from an eighteenth-century play—Mrs. Malaprop.

malodorous *(adj.)*
malˈōdərəs
Foul-smelling.

malady *(n.)* malədē
An illness.

malice *(n.)* maləs
Hatred.

malign *(v.)* məˈlīn
To say bad things about, slander.

maleficent *(adj.)*
məlefəsənt
Evil.

ACTIVITY 122

Provide the word for the given definition:

1. hatred = _____

2. to slander = _____

3. evil = _____

4. unintended comical misuse of a word = _____

5. foul-smelling = _____

6. a disease carried by mosquitoes = _____

7. an illness = _____

8. wrongdoing = _____

Prefix: *Phon-*

These words utilize the root *phon-*, meaning "sound."

telephone *(n.)* teləˌfōn
Literally "distant sound" (think of *telepathy*, or the ability to read minds).

You've probably heard *telephone* countless times. But you might not have known that it relies on the root *tele-*, meaning "distant," and *phon-*, meaning "sound."

phonetic *(adj.)* fəˈnetik
Relating to the way words are spoken.

*He was able to learn Spanish **phonetically**, listening to how it was spoken without having to rely on a book.*

From the Greek for "speak." Phonetic languages, in which letters correspond to specific sounds, are generally much easier to learn than languages in which symbols have no bearing on how the word sounds.

cacophony *(n.)* kəˈkäfənē
A harsh sound.

*As soon as the judge read the verdict, nobody could hear what he said next, so loud was the **cacophony**.*

This word comes from the Greek for "bad sound." *Cacophonous* is the adjective form of this word.

symphony *(n.)* simfənē
A large group of instruments creating music.

homophone *(n.)*
ˈhäməˌfōn
A word that sounds exactly like another word but has a different meaning and is often spelled differently.

francophone *(n.)*
fraNGkəˌfōn
A French speaker.

anglophone *(n.)*
aNGgləˌfōn
An English speaker.

phoneme *(n.)* fōnēm
A unit of sound in a language.

ACTIVITY 123

Provide the word for the given definition:

1. relating to the way words are spoken = _____

2. a French speaker = _____

3. a word that sounds the same as another but has a different meaning = _____

4. a harsh sound = _____

5. an English speaker = _____

6. a unit of sound in a language = _____

Prefix: *Eu-*

The words on this list turn to *eu-*, a different root meaning "good."

euphoria *(n.)* yo͞oˈfôrēə
An extreme feeling of happiness and joy.

*Upon finding out that she was one of three winners of the jackpot, she was flooded with a feeling of **euphoria**.*

From the Greek for "born well, healthy." The adjective form of the word is *euphoric*.

euphemism *(n.)* yo͞ofəˌmizəm
A pleasant way of saying or describing something that is unpleasant.

*When she described him as a creative golfer she was using a **euphemism**; he rarely kept the ball on the green.*

Another word from Greek meaning to "use auspicious words." Other euphemisms include "kick the bucket," "adult beverage," and "use the restroom."

eugenics *(n.)* yo͞oˈjeniks
Controlled breeding to increase desirable heritable characteristics in people.

*The pernicious idea of **eugenics** has caused much suffering.*

From the Greek for "well born." This was, and continues to be, a controversial theory. It's important to know this word, as it often comes up in discussions about the ethics of genetic technology.

euthanasia *(n.)*
yo͞oTHəˈnāZH(ē)ə
The practice of inducing painless death in a person or animal too sick to live.

eulogy *(n.)* yo͞oləjē
A speech of praise, typically at a funeral.

eureka *(interjection)*
yo͞oˈrēkə
An exclamation of joy upon discovering something.

euphony *(n.)* yo͞ofənē
Harmonious, pleasant sound.

eudaemonic *(adj.)*
yo͞odəˈmänik
Promoting happiness.

ACTIVITY 124

Provide the word for the given definition:

1. a speech of praise at a funeral = _____

2. harmonious sound = _____

3. an exclamation of joy upon discovering something = _____

4. a pleasant way of describing something unpleasant = _____

5. the practice of inducing painless death = _____

Prefix: *Anthro-*

All these words are centered upon the Greek root *anthro-*, meaning "man."

anthropology *(n.)* anθrəˈpäləjē
The study of humankind.

*The **anthropology** major decided to spend the summer in Papua New Guinea, studying a forest tribe that had been "discovered" only a few years earlier.*

Literally "man study." Cultural anthropologists spend time learning about a specific people, whereas physical anthropologists try to understand how humans evolved.

anthropocentric *(adj.)* anθrəpōˈsentrik
Viewing humankind as the center of the universe.

*If we are alone in the universe, an **anthropocentric** stance seems reasonable, but even the existence of one alien species would cast our primacy into doubt.*

Literally "man center." The noun form of *anthropocentric* is *anthropocentrism*.

anthropomorphic *(adj.)* anθrəpəˈmôrfik
Taking on human characteristics.

*Her art is abstract yet familiar, creating shapes that walk the line between the symbolic and the **anthropomorphic**.*

Literally "man shape." The noun form of *anthropomorphic* is *anthropomorphism*.

anthropogenic *(adj.)*
anθrəpōˈjenik
Induced or altered by humans.

anthropophagy *(n.)*
anθrəˈpäfəjē
Cannibalism.

Anthropocene *(n.)*
ˈanTHrəpəˌsēn
The current geological age.

ACTIVITY 125

Write the word that completes each sentence:

1. Climate scientists maintain that much global warming is _____, or created by people.

2. The study of people, or _____, is becoming less popular as a college major.

3. In the last 200 or so years, we have been living in the _____ era.

4. Most religions are not _____ because they do not believe that humans are the center of the universe.

5. The human brain is wired for _____, perceiving faces among chaos ("the man on the moon" being one example).

Prefix: *Circum-*

These terms all use the root *circum-*, meaning "around."

circumspect *(adj.)* sərkəmˌspekt
Cautious.

After a week in the jungle, the trekkers had become **circumspect**, *always scanning the ground for snakes before taking a step.*

Literally "to look around." *Chary* and *cautious* are synonyms.

circumvent *(v.)* sərkəmˈvent
To figure out a way around an obstacle.

Some citizens have **circumvented** *the ordinance against putting garbage in the recycling bin by putting the garbage in first and then covering it with recyclables.*

Literally "go around." This word is often part of the phrase "circumvent the law/rules regarding [something]."

circumscribe *(v.)* sərkəmˌskrīb
To set limits to.

Whereas the townsfolk had once roamed free, the recent gang violence **circumscribed** *their daily routines so that they were never far from their homes.*

From the Latin "to make a circle around."

circumlocution *(n.)*
sərkəmˌlōˈkyo͞oSHən
An indirect way
of speaking.

circumstance *(n.)*
sərkəmˌstans
A fact or condition
connected to an event
or action.

circumambulate *(v.)*
sərkəmˈambyəˌlāt
To walk around something.

circumference *(n.)*
sərˈkəmf(ə)rən(t)s
The perimeter of a circle.

ACTIVITY 126

Provide the word for the given definition:

1. to walk around something = _____

2. to set limits or boundaries = _____

3. an indirect way of speaking = _____

4. the perimeter of a circle = _____

5. to figure out a way to get around an obstacle = _____

Suffix: -Cracy

Words on this list end in *–cracy*, which means "rule."

bureaucracy *(n.)* byo͞oˈräkrəsē
Rule by state officials.

*The country is highly **bureaucratic**, so it can take months to get a visa to travel there.*

This comes from French and Greek for "desk rule." This form of rule involves an elaborate hierarchy of individuals, which can often delay simple procedures.

autocracy *(n.)* ôˈtäkrəsē
A dictatorship.

*Not all **autocracies** are malevolent; in fact, some are benign as long as the prevailing order goes unchallenged.*

Comes from the Greek for "rule by oneself." The adjective *autocratic* (a word from an earlier lesson) describes a ruler who governs with absolute power or anybody who rules in a highly domineering fashion.

plutocracy *(n.)* plo͞oˈtäkrəsē
Rule by the wealthy.

*As the gap between rich and poor widens, many decry our government as a **plutocracy**.*

This is from the Greek for "wealth rule" (power of the wealthy). This word does not relate to Pluto, the dwarf planet or the Greek god of the underworld.

democracy *(n.)*
dəˈmäkrəsē
Rule by the people.

aristocracy *(n.)*
erəˈstäkrəsē
Rule by the elite.

theocracy *(n.)* THēˈäkrəsē
Rule by a specific religion.

technocracy *(n.)*
tekˈnäkrəsē
Rule by those who control technology.

gerontocracy *(n.)*
jerənˈtäkrəsē
Rule by old people.

ACTIVITY 127

Provide the word for the given original meaning:

1. "god rule" = _____

2. "people rule" = _____

3. "elite rule" = _____

4. "wealthy rule" = _____

5. "desk rule" = _____

6. "old rule" = _____

Prefix: *Di-*

Words here begin with *di-*, meaning "two."

dichotomy *(n.)* dīˈkätəmē
A splitting of things into two distinct groups.

*The **dichotomy** between art and technology is not as clear-cut as we think—take the latest smartphone, for instance, which combines elegance with function.*

Comes from the Greek for "two cut." The study of the human body—*anatomy*, which shares the root *-tomy*—literally means "to cut up."

dilate *(v.)* dīˌlāt
To enlarge or open up.

*Our pupils **dilate** in response to light.*

This comes from Late Latin via Old French and originally meant "apart wide." The adjective *dilatory* means "slow" and "taking one's time."

diurnal *(adj.)* dīˈərn
Occurring or active during the day.

*Humans tend to be **diurnal** creatures, as anyone who has ever worked a night shift can tell you.*

From the Latin for "day," and not related to the root. Though this word isn't related to the root for "two," it can easily be mistaken as such, so it is included here so you can be aware of the difference.

diverse *(adj.)* diˈvərs
Having great variety.

diverge *(v.)* diˈvərj
To move in different directions, in terms of growth.

dissect *(v.)* diˈsekt
To cut in two.

dilute *(v.)* diˈlōot
To make something less concentrated.

ACTIVITY 128

Provide the word for the given definition:

1. active during the day = _____

2. a splitting of things into two different groups = _____

3. to move in different directions = _____

4. to cut in two = _____

5. to enlarge = _____

6. having great variety = _____

Prefix: *Dia-*

Words on this list feature the root *dia-*, meaning "through."

diameter *(n.)* dīˈamitər
The distance between two points at opposite ends of a circle.

*The **diameter** of the Frisbee used in Ultimate tournaments is 10.75 inches.*

Originally from the Greek for "measure across." Half of the *diameter* is known as the *radius.*

diagnosis *(n.)* dīəgˈnōsis
The determination of a cause of illness.

*The doctor's **diagnosis** of the patient's mysterious rash came as a relief: It was a harmless allergic reaction to an antibiotic.*

This is from the Greek for "a distinguishing." *Prognosis* is a similar word but describes not what is wrong but an estimate of how long recovery will take.

dialogue *(n.)* dīəˌläg
A conversation between two or more people or groups.

*The two warring nations are open to a **dialogue**, both hoping for an imminent cease-fire.*

This word comes from the Greek for "speak across." *Monologue* is a similar word, describing a conversation one has with oneself.

diorama *(n.)* dīəˈramə
A small model representing a scene in three dimensions.

diadem *(n.)* dīəˌdem
A jeweled crown.

diachronic *(adj.)* dīəˈkränik
Describing how something changes or evolves over time.

diapason *(n.)* dīəˈpāzən
A loud, rich burst of harmony.

ACTIVITY 129

Write the word that completes each sentence:

1. The princess wore a _____ to the coronation.

2. Phyllis made a _____ of the solar system for the science fair and won first place.

3. Pressing down all the keys on the organ, Charlie created a _____.

Unscramble each word and define:

4. auiegold _____

5. materide _____

6. signoadsi _____

Prefix: *Epi-*

These words build upon the root *epi-*, which means "upon."

epidemic *(n.)* epiˈdemik
An outbreak of a disease or something undesirable.

The car-theft **epidemic** *has abated significantly ever since street cameras were installed.*

From the Greek *epidemia* meaning "upon the people." The word *pandemic* (literally "all people") describes a disease that affects most of the population of an entire country, whereas *epidemic* is more localized.

epitome *(n.)* iˈpitəmē
The perfect example or embodiment of something.

He was the **epitome** *of a bad boss, yelling at his employees for no reason at all.*

This comes from the Greek for "an abridgement." *Embodiment* and *paragon* are two synonyms.

epistolary *(n.)* iˈpistəˌlerē
Relating to letter writing.

The book is in **epistolary** *form, each chapter a letter from a young man to his older self and vice versa.*

From the Latin word *epistola*, meaning "a letter." The *epistles* are the letters written by the apostle Paul to the churches of his time, and they form much of the New Testament.

epitaph *(n.)* epiˌtaf
A phrase written on a tombstone.

epithet *(n.)* epəˌθet
A word or phrase (typically negative) used to describe a person.

epigram *(n.)* epiˌgram
A short saying.

epigraph *(n.)* epiˌgraf
An inscription on a building, or a short quote at the beginning of a book.

ACTIVITY 130

Provide the word for the given definition:

1. relating to letter writing = _____

2. a word (typically negative) used to describe a person = _____

3. a short saying = _____

4. a phrase written on a tombstone = _____

5. an inscription on a building = _____

6. an outbreak of a disease = _____

7. the perfect example = _____

Prefix: *Ex-* (PART 1)

The following words begin with *ex-*, meaning "out."

extant *(adj.)* ekstənt
Still in existence (not used to refer to living things).

Extant recordings of great nineteenth-century musicians exist, though the quality is not very good.

This word comes from the Latin for "stand out." Though *extant* sounds somewhat like *extinct*, it is essentially the opposite. A good way to remember this word is to put an "is" between the *x* and the *t*, as in *ex(is)tant*, which sounds like *existent*.

exquisite *(adj.)* ekˈskwizit
Very beautiful but typically delicate.

*The ballerina starring as the swan had **exquisite** features.*

From the Latin for "sought out." This word can also mean "very precise" and "discerning" (e.g., the comedian had exquisite timing).

excommunicate *(v.)* ekskəˈmyo͞oniˌkāt
To banish or no longer allow a person to be part of a group.

*For questioning the legitimacy of the pope, the iconoclastic priest was **excommunicated**.*

Comes from the Latin for "not being able to communicate with the faithful." This word typically refers to the church's decision to remove or exclude somebody from taking part in church services.

exert *(v.)* igˈzərt
To put forth an effort.

exempt *(adj.)* igˈzem(p)t
Not having to fulfill a specific obligation.

exact *(v.)* igˈzakt
To demand payment.

excruciating *(adj.)*
ikˈskro͞oSHēˌātiNG
Extremely painful.

exemplar *(n.)* igˈzemplər
A perfect model or example of something.

ACTIVITY 131

Match the word with its meaning:

1. exert _____

2. exact _____

3. exempt _____

4. extant _____

5. excommunicate _____

6. exemplar _____

7. excruciating _____

a. to make an effort

b. still existing

c. to banish from the church

d. an ideal model

e. very painful

f. to require

g. not required

Prefix: *Ex-* (PART 2)

exhume *(v.)* igˈz(y)o͞om
To dig up out of the ground.

Sally and her friend had buried a toy jewelry box with a friendship bracelet and **exhumed** *it a year later to find it intact.*

This is from Medieval Latin for "out of earth." *Inter*, meaning "to bury," is the opposite of *exhume*, while *disinter* is a synonym.

exorcise *(v.)* eksôrˌsīz
To remove or purge something undesirable.

By lowering interest rates, the Fed has **exorcised** *any concerns that it would raise them.*

Comes from the Greek for "bind by oath." This word was originally used to refer to evil spirits (as in the movie *The Exorcist*), but today it is often used figuratively.

expatriate *(v.)* eksˈpātrēit
To move to a different country and settle there.

The group was **expatriated** *from Europe and now lives near the river.*

From the Latin for "out of native country." To *repatriate* means "to send someone back to their native country."

expedient *(adj.)*
ikˈspēdēənt
Convenient but not necessarily ethical.

expeditious *(adj.)*
ekspəˈdiSHəs
Acting with prompt efficiency.

expend *(v.)* ikˈspend
To exert or use up, as energy.

explicate *(v.)* ekspliˌkāt
To explain at length.

exploit *(v.)* ikˈsploit
To use, often in the sense of to take advantage of.

ACTIVITY 132

Write the word that completes each sentence:

1. For his term paper, he was able to _____ the resources available in his library.

2. She tried not to _____ her energy the night before the race.

3. The college professor was skillful at _____ many complex subjects.

4. Though it might be _____ not to come to a full stop at a stop sign, it is illegal.

5. She was _____ in terms of completing the task, finishing the book a month before the deadline.

6. In order to determine the identity of the victim using DNA analysis, they had to _____ the body.

7. He was able to _____ all his childhood fears about heights and climb up the rock wall.

Prefix: *Ex-* (PART 3)

exposé *(n.)* ekspōˈzā
A piece of usually sensational journalism that uncovers corruption and scandal.

*The **exposé** revealed what many in the town had long known: that the water running through the old mill was toxic.*

This word comes from French for "shown." Note the accent over the last *e*, which changes the sound to "ay" as in French; don't confuse the pronunciation with the verb *expose*.

extemporaneous *(adj.)* ikˌstempəˈrānēəs
Done with no preparation.

*Jared dreaded **extemporaneous** speeches after being asked in third grade to stand in front of the class and speak about his most embarrassing moment.*

From the Medieval Latin for "out of time." *Impromptu* is a common synonym.

expostulate *(v.)* ikˈspäsCHəˌlāt
To reason with, to plead.

*The man **expostulated** his displeasure about his neighbor's dog, which barked all night.*

This is from Latin, meaning "to demand." This word has been used less and less over the decades, and if you do indeed see it, it will likely be on a standardized test.

extort *(v.)* ikˈstôrt
To take money from by use of threats.

extradite *(v.)* ekstrəˌdīt
To bring a criminal back to the country to go on trial.

expository *(adj.)*
ikˈspäziˌtôrē
Relating to the act of explaining.

exult *(v.)* igˈzəlt
To express great joy.

extricate *(v.)* ekstriˌkāt
To remove from a difficult situation.

ACTIVITY 133

Match the word with its definition:

1. extort _____
2. extradite _____
3. exult _____
4. extemporaneous _____
5. expostulate _____
6. extricate _____
7. exposé _____

a. to express great joy

b. to bring a criminal back to the country to go on trial

c. to take money from by use of threats

d. to remove from a difficult situation

e. done with no preparation

f. to reason with

g. a piece of journalism uncovering corruption

Prefix: *Im-* (PART 1)

These words use the prefix *im-*, which can mean either "not" or "in." Since this root has two meanings, trying to apply these meanings can get you into trouble, because you might come up with the opposite of what the word actually signifies. I've therefore mixed the *im-* words meaning "in" and "not" together, so that you'll focus on learning the definition of these words rather than attempting to figure out their meaning based on the root.

imbibe *(v.)* imˈbīb
To drink or take in, whether literally or figuratively.

*She was an early riser, **imbibing** whole morning lectures but then nodding off in her afternoon class.*

This comes from the Latin for "drink in." This word is typically used to describe the drinking of alcohol.

impeach *(v.)* imˈpēCH
To charge with wrongdoing.

*The op-ed columnist **impeached** the business mogul's integrity, implying that all of his charity had been self-serving.*

This comes from the Latin for "entangle." To *impeach* a president does not mean to remove that person from power. Rather, it means to officially charge them with wrongdoing.

immerse *(v.)* iˈmərs
To put inside a medium or environment.

impair *(v.)* imˈpe(ə)r
To diminish the quality of something.

impart *(v.)* imˈpärt
To give knowledge to.

imbue *(v.)* imˈbyo͞o
To give a certain quality to.

ACTIVITY 134

Complete the word for the given definition:

1. im_____ = to drink or take in

2. im _____ = to give knowledge to

3. im_____ = to diminish the quality of

4. im_____ = to charge with wrongdoing

5. im_____ = to give a certain quality to

Prefix: *Im-* (PART 2)

impel *(v.)* imˈpel
To force somebody to do something.

*Keith's friends **impelled** him to walk up to his crush and ask her on a date, though he was unable to say anything beyond "Hey."*

Comes from the Latin for "drive forward." *Propel*, as in an abstract force (not a propeller) that drives someone forward, is a synonym.

impenetrable *(adj.)* imˈpenətrəbəl
Difficult, if not impossible, to understand.

*The work of James Joyce is **impenetrable** to many without the help of 300 pages of footnotes.*

This is from the Latin for "that cannot be penetrated." This word can also mean "something that cannot be passed through physically," as in an impenetrable jungle.

implausible *(adj.)* imˈplôzəbəl
Not believable.

*Once again, the tabloid featured an **implausible** story of an alien abduction.*

First used around 1677, meaning "not applauded." An informal way of saying this is "hard to swallow."

implore *(v.)* imˈplôr
To beg.

imponderable *(adj.)*
imˈpändərəbəl
Difficult to grasp.

impoverished *(adj.)*
imˈpäv(ə)risht
Deprived of money.

impuissant *(adj.)*
imˈpwisənt
Not powerful.

ACTIVITY 135

Unscramble the word and define:

1. lompier _____

2. plime _____

Write the word that completes each sentence:

3. The Great Depression left many _____.

4. Estimating the number of grains of sand that can fit inside the known universe is truly _____.

Prefix: *In-* (PART 1)

The words on this list use the Latin root *in-*. Like *im-*, this root can also mean "in" or "not."

inadvertent *(adj.)* inəd'vərtnt
Not done intentionally.

*He had an **inadvertent** encounter with a mouse in the kitchen, but luckily his wife came home and shooed it out.*

The first known use was in the 1650s and meant "not turning the mind to." *Unwitting* is a good synonym to know.

inculcate *(v.)* in'kəl͵kāt
To instill.

*Despite having **inculcated** healthy study habits in his three children, only the eldest routinely did her homework.*

From the Latin for "tread on." This word is usually used in the context of instilling values or attitudes.

inamorata *(n.)* in͵amə'rätə
One's female lover.

*His **inamorata** wore many pieces of jewelry, all of which he had bought for her in the last year.*

From Italian meaning "in love." *Inamorato*, referring to a male lover, is not commonly used.

inane *(adj.)* i'nān
Silly, stupid.

inapt *(adj.)* i'napt
Not suitable or appropriate.

incandescent *(adj.)* inkən'desənt
Extremely hot and bright.

inadmissible *(adj.)* inəd'misəb(ə)l
Not acceptable, as in a courtroom.

ACTIVITY 136

Match the word with its meaning:

1. inane _____
2. inapt _____
3. inamorata _____
4. incandescent _____
5. inculcate _____
6. inadmissible _____
7. inadvertent _____

a. a female lover
b. to instill
c. not acceptable (legally)
d. not suitable
e. extremely hot and bright
f. silly
g. unintentional

Prefix: *In-* (PART 2)

incarcerate *(v.)* inˈkärsəˌrāt
To imprison.

*He'd been **incarcerated** several times before he was 25, when he finally turned his life around.*

From Medieval Latin meaning "into prison." This word is usually used formally and not much in conversation.

inclement *(adj.)* inˈklemənt
Describing harsh or unpleasant weather.

*The weather was so **inclement** that the championship game had to be postponed to the next day.*

From the Latin for "harsh." The word *clement* can describe mild weather (making it an antonym), though it can also describe somebody who is merciful.

incipient *(adj.)* inˈsipēənt
Just starting off, at the beginning stage.

*The **incipient** signs of a cold are a scratchy throat and a run-down feeling.*

Comes from Latin meaning "take in." Two fancy-sounding synonyms for this word are *embryonic* and *inchoate*.

incentivize *(v.)*
inˈsentəˌvīz
To provide rewards to stimulate one to action.

inception *(n.)* inˈsepSHən
Beginning.

incinerate *(v.)* inˈsinəˌrāt
To burn.

incite *(v.)* inˈsīt
To lead to an action, often negative.

ACTIVITY 137

Write the word that completes each sentence:

1. With so many more criminals being _____, prisons are becoming overly crowded.

2. The riot police quickly broke up the _____ chaos in the city square.

3. No evidence was left because everything had been _____ during the blaze.

Complete the word for the given definition:

4. inc__e = to lead to an action, often negative

5. inc___t = describing harsh or unpleasant weather

6. ince___ze = to provide rewards to stimulate one to action

Prefix: *In-* (PART 3)

incongruous *(adj.)* inˈkäNGgro͞oəs
Out of place when describing the surroundings.

The gleaming new building housing a trendy café felt **incongruous** *amid the old warehouses.*

This word comes from the Latin for "not agreeing." A similar meaning (and similar looking) word is *incongruent*.

inconsolable *(adj.)* inkənˈsōləbəl
Unable to be cheered up.

After his favorite sitcom character was written out of the show, Mark was **inconsolable** *for weeks.*

Again from Latin, this meant "not able to be consoled." *Distraught* and *despairing* are two good synonyms.

incorrigible *(adj.)* inˈkôrijəbəl
Unable to be changed or reformed, as a person's behavior.

Niles was an **incorrigible** *nail-biter, working his way through an entire thumb during a red light.*

From Latin via Old French and meaning "not to be corrected." A good synonym to know, and also an *in-* word, is *inveterate*.

incredulous *(adj.)*
inˈkrejələs
Not inclined to believing.

indiscriminate *(adj.)*
indiˈskrimənit
Without prior judgment.

incontrovertible *(adj.)*
inˌkäntrəˈvərtəbəl
Unable to be disproven or challenged.

ACTIVITY 138

Write the word that completes each sentence:

1. He was an _____ liar, knowing full well that lying was wrong yet unable to control himself.

2. Carol was _____ when it came to dining out, looking simply for a place that would sate her hunger.

3. The crowd was _____ that the aging opera star was able to hit a high C, a note he had been unable to hit in years.

4. That the Earth is not flat seems _____, though there are still people who claim otherwise.

Prefix: *In-* (PART 4)

indulgent *(adj.)* inˈdəljənt
Ready to treat someone very leniently.

*Even after she promised to ground Cooper for a week, his mother was usually **indulgent** and within an hour, he would be outside with his friends again.*

Another word from Latin, meaning "kind, tender, fond."
Self-indulgent describes one who focuses on enjoying themselves whenever they feel like it.

ineffable *(adj.)* inˈefəbəl
Impossible to describe or to put into words.

*The volcano eruption had turned the sky all different types of colors, and the sunsets were simply **ineffable** (unless you were a gifted poet).*

This is from Latin via Old French, meaning "not utter." *Effable* is also a word, but it is rarely used.

indoctrinate *(v.)*
inˈdäktrəˌnāt
To fill someone with specific teachings.

infectious *(adj.)*
inˈfekSHəs
Easily spread.

inter *(v.)* inˈtər
To bury.

inequity *(n.)* inˈekwitē
The lack of equality.

ACTIVITY 139

Match the word with its meaning:

1. inequity _____

2. indoctrinate _____

3. indulgent _____

4. infectious _____

5. inter _____

6. ineffable _____

a. unable to be put into words

b. contagious

c. the opposite of *exhume*

d. overly lenient

e. unfairness

f. to fill with a particular ideology

Prefix: *In-* (PART 5)

inimical *(adj.)* iˈnimikəl
Hostile.

*The desert sun was **inimical** to healthy skin—unless you protected your face, you'd develop fine wrinkles.*

From the Latin for "enemy." *Deleterious* and *antagonistic* are synonyms.

iniquity *(n.)* iˈnikwitē
Unfair or immoral behavior.

*The tyrant smiled for the press, but his **iniquity** was well known among his subjects.*

From the Latin for "not just." *Iniquitous* is the adjective form.

insinuate *(v.)* inˈsinyəˌwāt
To imply something negative, usually in an indirect but nasty way.

*The prosecution **insinuated** that the defendant had been at the scene of the crime, pointing out that she never came home that night.*

This is again from Latin, meaning "introduce curved and winding." *Insinuate* can also mean "to insert oneself into a social situation, conversation."

incapacitate *(v.)*
inkəˈpasiˌtāt
To take away the ability from.

inhibit *(v.)* inˈhibit
To decrease or slow down.

innumerable *(adj.)* iˈn(y) o͞omərəbəl
Too many to be counted.

instigate *(v.)* instiˌgāt
To start something, usually bad.

ACTIVITY 140

Match the word with its meaning:

1. insinuate _____

2. iniquity _____

3. inhibit _____

4. incapacitate _____

5. instigate _____

6. inimical _____

7. innumerable _____

a. too great to count

b. hostile

c. to take away the ability

d. to start something bad

e. something highly corrupt and unfair

f. to hold back

g. to subtly imply something unkind

Prefix: *Inter-* (PART 1)

Below are words beginning with *inter-*, meaning "between" or "among."

intersperse *(v.)* intər'spərs
To scatter among or mix throughout.

*His speech was **interspersed** with chuckles as he laughed at his own jokes.*

From Latin for "scattered between." *Interspersion* is the noun form, though it is not very common.

interrogate *(v.)* in'terə,gāt
To question, usually in an aggressive manner.

*The witness was **interrogated** relentlessly in court but never lost her composure.*

This comes from the Latin for "ask in between." *Interrogation* is the noun form.

intercede *(v.)* intər'sēd
To interfere on another's behalf.

*As a pro bono lawyer, she always **interceded** on behalf of the poor.*

From the Latin for "go in between." *Intercession* is the noun form, though this word is not very common.

interdict *(v.)* intər,dikt
To prohibit.

interim *(n.)* 'intərəm
An intervening time period.

interject *(v.)* intər'jekt
To say something while someone else is talking.

ACTIVITY 141

Write the word that completes each sentence:

1. When the star pupil realized the teacher's math on the board was wrong, she tried to _____, but the teacher carried on.

2. The witness was _____ relentlessly.

3. Nobody was able to _____ when the fight broke out, and it only escalated.

Complete the word for the given definition:

4. in_____ = to prohibit

5. in_____ = an intervening period

6. in_____ = to scatter throughout

Prefix: *Inter-* (PART 2)

intermediary *(n.)* intərˈmēdēˌerē
Somebody who acts as a go-between for people.

Since the two neighbors were no longer speaking, a third had to act as an **intermediary**.

From the Latin for "the thing in between." Good synonyms include *go-between* and *mediator*.

interloper *(n.)* intərˌlōpər
An intruder.

Though he had pretended to know the groom, the man in the cheap gray suit turned out to be an **interloper**, *crashing the wedding for free food.*

From a Dutch word meaning "vagabond." *Trespasser* is another way to think of this word.

interlocutor *(n.)* intərˈläkyətər
A person engaged in a conversation.

He was engaged in lively debate with three **interlocutors** *when somebody's phone rang.*

From the Latin for "speak in between." This word is very formal.

intermission *(n.)*
intərˈmiSHən
A small pause, typically at the halfway point of a long theatrical production.

interplay *(n.)* intərˌplā
The interaction of different factors.

internecine *(adj.)*
intərˈnesēn
Describing conflict within a group.

ACTIVITY 142

Match the word with its meaning:

1. interlocutor _____
2. intermission _____
3. internecine _____
4. interplay _____
5. interloper _____
6. intermediary _____

a. a go-between
b. regarding in-group conflict
c. interaction of different factors
d. an intruder
e. a pause in a long work
f. a person engaged in a conversation

Prefix: *Sub-*

These words begin with the prefix *sub-*, meaning "below."

subservient *(adj.)* səbˈsərvēənt
Slavish.

*Lord Watkins preferred chatty butlers to those who were **subservient** and merely carried out his every wish with a "Yes, sir."*

This word comes from the Latin for "going along with, complying." This word is different from *obsequious*, which implies somebody who acts excessively subservient but who also has an agenda (e.g., they want a higher-up to like them).

submerge *(v.)* səbˈmərj
To go underwater.

*After three days of intense rain, the doghouse outside became **submerged**.*

Comes from the Latin for "dip under." This word can also be used figuratively, to mean that something obscured or hid another, as in hatred submerged beneath a fake smile.

subsume *(v.)* səbˈso͞om
To encompass, include.

*Many successful Internet start-ups end up being **subsumed** by a larger corporation.*

From the Latin for "take below." This verb is often used intransitively, i.e., be subsumed.

subterranean *(adj.)*
səbtəˈrānēən
Underground.

subservient *(adj.)*
səbˈsərvēənt
Slavish.

subsidize *(v.)* səbsəˌdīz
To pay for or fund part of a larger expense.

substantiate *(v.)*
səbˈstanCHēˌāt
To give more validity or legitimacy to by offering evidence.

ACTIVITY 143

Match the word with its meaning:

1. subjugate _____
2. submerge _____
3. substantiate _____
4. subsidize _____
5. subterranean _____
6. subsume _____
7. subservient _____

a. inclined to serve
b. to back up with evidence
c. to plunge into water
d. to encompass
e. underground
f. to make submissive
g. to pay part of a large expense

Root: -*Pathy*

These words contain the root -*pathy*, meaning "feeling."

empathy *(n.)* empəθē
The understanding of another's feelings without having the feelings fully communicated.

*She felt **empathy** with her boyfriend when his dog died because she too had lost a pet.*

Comes from the Greek for "state of emotion." There are two adjective forms of this word, *empathetic* and *empathic*, which should not be confused with *emphatic*, meaning "done with emphasis."

apathy *(n.)* apəθē
Lack of emotion or lack of caring.

*Philip was known for his **apathy**; few things excited him.*

This is from a Greek word meaning "want of sensation." The adjective form of this word, which is perhaps more common than the noun form, is *apathetic*.

antipathy *(n.)* anˈtipəθē
Strong dislike or aversion.

*He had an **antipathy** for large crowds and avoided taking public transportation, especially during rush hour.*

Again from Greek, meaning "feeling against." A good related word to know is *animosity*, which is perhaps even a touch more extreme, reserved only for those instances when someone is really hostile toward something.

sociopath *(n.)* sōsēōˌpaθ
A person who struggles to relate to others and essentially has no conscience, or feels no guilt about harming others.

pathogen *(n.)*
paθəjən;
Something that causes sickness or disease.

pathos *(n.)* pāˌθäs
A feeling of sadness.

pathological *(adj.)*
paθəˈläjikəl
Relating to disease or to a habitual behavior.

homeopathic *(adj.)*
hōmēˈäpəθik
Describing remedies in which a smaller dose of whatever is causing the sickness or illness is administered.

ACTIVITY 144

Match the word with its meaning:

1. a feeling of sadness _____

2. something that causes disease _____

3. having to do with disease _____

4. a person with no conscience _____

5. not caring _____

6. strong dislike _____

7. ability to relate to another person's emotions _____

a. antipathy

b. sociopath

c. apathetic

d. empathy

e. pathos

f. pathogen

g. pathological

Root: *Fract-, Frag-*

These words are based on the root *fract-* or *frag-*, meaning "broken."

refractory *(adj.)* ri'fraktərē
Poorly behaved, stubborn.

*The children were **refractory** with the new nanny, pointedly disobeying everything she said.*

Comes from the Latin for "obstinate." This is a similar word to *obstreperous* and *recalcitrant*, two words you typically don't see outside of a standardized test or a nineteenth-century English novel.

fractious *(adj.)* frakSHəs
Difficult to control or manage.

*The new political party was **fractious**, so it didn't surprise many that a strong-armed dictator emerged as its leader.*

The origin of this word is related to the Latin word for "rupture, discord." A similar-sounding word but one with a slightly different meaning is *factious*, which means "likely to split into groups."

fragment *(n.)* fragmənt
A small piece of something that has broken off.

*Archaeologists have been able to determine from mere **fragments** of pottery what ancient peoples likely ate on a daily basis.*

From the Latin for "a remnant." This word can also be used figuratively to describe isolated and scattered bits of something—e.g., "She recalled fragments of her dream throughout the day."

fragile *(adj.)* frajəl
Very delicate, likely to break.

fracture *(v.)* frakCHər
To break, either literally or figuratively.

fractal *(n.)* fraktəl
A pattern (typically in nature) that is repeated at widely different scales of size.

ACTIVITY 145

Write the word that completes each sentence:

1. Timmy _____ his arm falling from the tree.

2. The vase is _____ and needs to be handled with care.

3. Many _____ of papyrus scrolls exist that give us a window into the life of the Egyptians.

Complete the word for the given definition:

4. poorly behaved, stubborn: re_____tory

5. difficult to control: ____act____

Prefix: *Bell-*

These words begin with *bell-*, meaning "war."

belligerent *(adj.)* bəˈlijərənt
Warlike, hostile.

*He was highly agreeable when he had his way, but as soon as someone disagreed with him he turned **belligerent**.*

This word comes from the Latin for "waging war." This word can also be used as a noun to refer to a nation that is constantly waging war.

bellow *(v.)* belō
To laugh loudly and deeply.

*His uncle **bellowed** at every joke he heard, even ones involving bad puns.*

From an Old English word. This word is actually not related to the root *bell-*, though many assume that it somehow relates to war.

bellicose *(adj.)* beliˌkōs
Hostile, inclined to fight.

*The newspaper gained a reputation as politically extreme after hiring several **bellicose** writers.*

Comes from the Latin for "warlike." *Pugnacious* and *truculent* are two synonyms.

belle *(n.)* bel
A beautiful girl (from the Latin *bellus-* for beautiful, not *bell-* for war).

antebellum *(adj.)*
antēˈbeləm
Before the Civil War.

casus belli *(n.)*
käsəs ˈbelē
A justification or reason for war.

ACTIVITY 146

Provide the word for the given definition:

1. hostile (2 words) = _____ and _____

2. a justification for war = _____

3. occurring or describing life before the Civil War = _____

4. a beautiful girl = _____

5. to laugh heartily = _____

Prefix: *Carn-*

This list of words is based on the root *carn-*, meaning "flesh."

carnal *(adj.)* kärnl
Relating to the body, specifically as it concerns sexual desire.

*The more **carnal** portions of the book were omitted in the movie adaptation, which had a PG-13 rating.*

This word is from the Latin for "of the flesh." The noun form of this word is *carnality*.

carnage *(n.)* kärnij
Bloodshed and killing on a grand scale.

*World history textbooks are filled with descriptions of **carnage**.*

Comes from the Latin for "a piece of flesh" then from Old Italian for "slaughter, murder." *Slaughter* is a synonym for *carnage*.

carnivore *(n.)* kärnəˌvôr
An animal that eats meat.

*The steak restaurant billed itself a **carnivore's** paradise, offering mashed potatoes as the only dish that didn't once stand on four legs.*

From the Latin for "flesh eating." An omnivore is one who eats everything (from the Latin *omni-* for all).

carnelian *(n.)* kärˈnēlyən
A semiprecious stone with a flesh-colored appearance.

carnation *(n.)* kärˈnāSHən
A pink, flesh-colored flower.

carnival *(n.)* kärnəvəl
A period of intense celebration and indulgence.

ACTIVITY 147

Match the word with its meaning:

1. meat eater _____
2. celebratory festival _____
3. a semiprecious stone _____
4. massive bloodshed _____
5. relating to desires of the body _____

a. carnivore
b. carnal
c. carnage
d. carnelian
e. carnival

Prefix: *Cogn-*

These words build upon the root *cogn-*, meaning "to learn."

cognitive *(adj.)* kägnətiv
Related to the mind.

*Her **cognitive** powers were truly amazing: By age 9 she had memorized pi to the one-thousandth decimal place and could recite T. S. Eliot's poem "The Waste Land."*

From the Latin for "to know." Cognitive science studies how the human brain processes information.

reconnaissance *(n.)* riˈkänəzəns
A preliminary military investigation.

*Before choosing a city to move its headquarters to, the corporation did some extensive **reconnaissance**, visiting dozens of towns.*

From the French word for "to recognize." *Recon* is a shortened, and informal, form of the word *reconnaissance*.

incognito *(adj.)* inkägˈnētō
In disguise, in order to avoid detection.

*The famous celebrity was known to go about town **incognito**, often donning a Panama hat and a fake moustache.*

This word is from the Latin for "not known." This word can also be used as a noun describing the false identity itself, though this usage is not nearly as common as the adjective case. That said, the word can also function as an adverb, e.g., *to go incognito*, and this form is relatively common.

recognize *(v.)* rekigˌnīz
To acknowledge.

cognizant *(adj.)*
kägnəzənt
Aware.

precognition *(n.)*
prēkägˈniSHən
The knowledge of something before it happens.

reconnoiter *(v.)*
rēkəˈnoitər
To inspect and learn about an area (usually the enemy's).

ACTIVITY 148

Write the word that completes each sentence:

1. The Navy Seal team _____ enemy territory weeks early, but their _____ did not reveal any unambiguous threats.

2. Many claim to have _____ of events before those events happen, though no one has ever been able to reveal such an ability when tested by scientists.

3. The culprit, in order to avoid being recognized, dressed _____.

4. _____ decline is a natural part of the aging process.

Root: *Min-*

These words use the root *min-*, meaning "to make smaller."

minimalism *(n.)* minəmə͵lizəm
An artistic movement that strives for simplicity.

*Influenced by **minimalism**, her paintings contained little more than a few lines and stray shapes, though the overall effect was striking.*

Minimalism doesn't just refer to painting and sculpture but can also describe music that repeats the same phrase over and over again, thereby creating a hypnotic effect.

minuscule *(adj.)* minə͵skyo͞ol
Extremely tiny or small.

*The difference between 1 light-year and 1.5 light-years might seem **minuscule**, but the actual difference is billions upon billions of miles.*

This is from the Latin for "rather small, rather less." Be careful not to spell this word *miniscule*, which is not correct but a tempting misspelling given the sense of *mini*.

minutiae *(n.)* mə'n(y)o͞oSHē͵ē
Tiny, trivial details.

*The **minutiae** of her daily commute became so embedded in her mind that when a small exit sign had been repainted, she immediately noticed it.*

From the Latin for "smallness." *Minutia* is the singular form but is rarely used.

diminish *(v.)* di'minish
To decrease in size or effect.

minute *(adj.)* mī'n(y)o͞ot
Very small and detailed.

diminution *(n.)* dimə'n(y)o͞oSHən
A lowering in rank or quality.

minatory *(adj.)* minə͵tôrē
Threatening (this word has a different root and is not related to the other words in this lesson).

ACTIVITY 149

Write the word that completes each sentence:

1. A _____ in his powers of concentration was evident at the three-hour mark of the chess game.

2. Though the lion was in a cage, its _____ glare was enough to frighten even the adults present.

3. Somebody with perfect pitch can identify even _____ shifts in tone.

4. He was a _____ member of the community and was recognized by many.

5. Many experts prognosticate that a housing crisis is _____.

Prefix: *Apo-*

These words begin with the prefix *apo-*, meaning "away from."

apocalypse *(n.)* əˈpäkəˌlips
The end times, or any catastrophe.

The storm was causing damage so extensive that many newspapers covering the story were describing it as an apocalypse.

This is from the Greek for "uncover." This word is usually used figuratively to describe any catastrophic events.

apostle *(n.)* əˈpäsəl
One who is a follower of another figure and typically spreads that figure's message.

He was an early apostle of the powers of the Internet, speaking as early as 1995 about the Web's potential to transform our lives.

Comes from the Greek for "person sent forth." *Apostle* can also mean "a supporter of a certain cause or idea" (see example sentence).

apogee *(n.)* apəjē
The point in its orbit at which the moon is farthest away from Earth, or any apex.

To many art historians, the period between Da Vinci and Rembrandt was the apogee of Western art.

From the Greek "away from the Earth." This word is also used to describe the highest point in the development of something (see example sentence).

apothecary *(n.)*
əˈpäθiˌkerē
A pharmacist.

apoplectic *(adj.)*
apəˈplektik
Extremely angry.

apologist *(n.)* əˈpäləjist
One who defends a controversial idea.

apothegm *(n.)* apəˌθem
A saying.

apotheosis *(n.)*
əˌpäθēˈōsis
The idealization of something or someone, the perfect instance of something.

ACTIVITY 150

Match the word with its meaning:

1. a saying _____

2. extremely angry _____

3. a perfect embodiment of something _____

4. a pharmacist _____

5. the highest point in something _____

6. defender of a controversial position _____

7. catastrophe _____

a. apocalypse

b. apothecary

c. apogee

d. apologist

e. apothegm

f. apoplectic

g. apotheosis

Root: -*Mit*

Words below are based on the root -*mit*, meaning "to send."

omit *(v.)* ōˈmit
To leave out, not include.

*She **omitted** details of her alibi that she had earlier mentioned to police, thereby arousing suspicion.*

This is from the Latin for "to let go." *Omission* is the noun form.

emit *(v.)* iˈmit
To send out.

*The pulsar **emitted** a light that radio telescopes were able to detect.*

Comes from the Latin for "to send forth." Do not confuse this word with *omit*. *Emit* can be used to describe an action more passive than *transmit*.

manumit *(v.)* manyəˈmit
To release from slavery or captivity.

*Very few captured by the Romans were lucky enough to be **manumitted**.*

Comes from the Latin for "send from one's hand." This term is formal and usually isn't encountered outside of history texts.

unremitting *(adj.)*
ənriˈmiting
Not ending, constant.

noncommittal *(adj.)*
nänkəˈmitl
Unwilling to make a decision or to commit oneself.

transmit *(v.)* tranzˈmit
To intentionally send or emit.

ACTIVITY 151

Match the word with its meaning:

1. to release someone from servitude _____

2. unending _____

3. to intentionally send _____

4. to leave out _____

5. not committing oneself _____

6. to send out _____

a. manumit

b. unremitting

c. transmit

d. omit

e. emit

f. noncommittal

Prefix: *Pan-*

Words below come from the root *pan-*, meaning "all."

panacea *(n.)* panəˈsēə
A cure-all.

Many politicians peddle the usual panaceas, but few ever deliver even half of what they promise.

This is from the Latin word for a herb that would heal all illnesses. The term *magic bullet* is a good way of thinking about a panacea.

pandemonium *(n.)* pandəˈmōnēəm
Complete chaos and disorder.

When the home team came from behind to win the final game of the series, the streets were pure pandemonium, with revelers rejoicing.

From a Latin word meaning "all demon," this was the name of the city in the center of hell, according to John Milton's *Paradise Lost*. *Bedlam* is a similar word and one with an interesting backstory: It was the name of a hospital for the insane.

panegyric *(n.)* panəˈjirik
Public praise, usually before a large crowd.

The dean was fond of giving a few panegyrics at graduation, referring to several students who had truly made a difference in the school.

This comes from the Greek word for "all assembly," referring to the public aspect of this word. This word can also refer to praise in writing. This is a pretty fancy word, but an even more formal synonym is *encomium*.

pantomime *(n.)*
pantəˌmīm
To use only gestures to communicate information.

pantheist *(n.)* panθēˌist
A person who believes that there is an all-pervading spirit or mind.

pandemic *(n.)* panˈdemik
A disease that breaks out in a large area.

panoply *(n.)* panəplē
A full, lavish display of something.

panopticon *(n.)*
paˈnäptiˌkän
A surveillance tower in a prison, from which the entire prison is visible to the guards.

ACTIVITY 152

Write the word that completes each sentence:

1. The influenza _____ of 1917 killed more people worldwide than the number of lives lost in World War I.

2. The baron enjoyed showing guests his _____ of art relics, ranging from Aztec to Celtic pieces.

3. The dictator loved being praised and so had "writers" pen daily _____.

4. There is no _____ for the many problems that plague that small nation.

5. The riot was pure _____, with businesses being looted and bystanders being injured.

Prefix: *Para-*

These words feature the root *para-*, meaning "beside."

paradox *(n.)* parə͵däks
A statement that doesn't seem genuine on the surface but is, in fact, true.

If one believed that nice guys finish last, he was a walking **paradox**— *a successful CEO of multiple companies who had a heart of gold.*

This comes from Greek, meaning "contrary opinion." This word can also refer to any situation or person that is contradictory.

paradigm *(n.)* parə͵dīm
A model or system that is the basis for a way of investigating or understanding the world.

Until recently, the medical establishment had discounted the role of the microbiome, the myriad bacteria in each one of us; but now the **paradigm** *includes these tiny species when trying to understand why people become sick and why they stay healthy.*

Also from Greek, meaning "show side by side." The term *paradigm shift* refers to a different way of thinking about something.

paroxysm *(n.)* parək͵sizəm
A sudden explosion of emotion.

At the political debate, a highly polarized audience burst into **paroxysms** *of joy one moment and anger the next.*

Comes from the Greek to "sharpen beyond." *Spasm* is a similar word to *paroxysm*.

paragon *(n.)* parə͵gän
The perfect example of something.

parabola *(n.)* pəˈrabələ
A figure that describes the path of any thrown object.

paralegal *(n.)* parəˈlēgəl
A person whose job it is to aid lawyers in legal matters.

paramount *(adj.)* parə͵mount
Of greatest importance.

parapet *(n.)* parəpit
A defensive wall behind which troops hide.

ACTIVITY 153

Match the word with its meaning:

1. sudden explosion of emotion _____

2. a defensive wall _____

3. of greatest importance _____

4. a person involved in legal matters but not a lawyer _____

5. contradictory statement _____

6. model used when studying something _____

a. parapet

b. paralegal

c. paradigm

d. paradox

e. paroxysm

f. paramount

Prefix: *Peri-*

Words on this list use the prefix *peri-*, meaning "around."

peripheral *(adj.)* pəˈrifərəl
Not of main importance, to the side.

Once war seemed imminent, all other issues in the media became *peripheral*.

From the Greek for "circumference." This word can also describe a physical location, as in "The periphery of the mountain was dotted with tiny villages."

peripatetic *(adj.)* peripəˈtetik
Moving around on foot.

In some dense urban areas, certain doctors are still *peripatetic*, *making house calls on foot.*

This comes from the Greek, meaning "walking up and down." This word comes from an ancient Greek school in which the philosophers would "hold class" by walking around and discussing ideas.

perigee *(n.)* perəˌjē
The point at which the moon is closest to Earth.

During the *perigee*, *the moon will appear brighter than usual.*

This is from Late Greek, meaning "near the Earth." Unlike *apogee*, this word has no figurative usage.

periscope *(n.)* perəˌskōp
A device that allows occupants of a submarine to see to the surface of the water.

periodontal *(adj.)*
ˌperēəˈdäntl
Relating to the structures around the teeth.

perihelion *(n.)*
perəˈhēlyən
The point at which Earth is closest to the sun.

periphrastic *(adj.)*
perəˈfrastik
Long-winded, not straightforward.

ACTIVITY 154

Complete the word for the given definition:

1. peri_____ = a device that allows occupants of a submarine to see to the surface

2. peri_____ = relating to the structures around the teeth

3. peri_____ = point at which the moon is closest to Earth

4. peri_____ = point at which Earth is closest to the sun

5. peri_____ = long-winded, not straightforward

6. peri_____ = not of main importance, to the side

Root: -*Scribe*, -*Script*

These words are all based on the root -*scribe* or -*script* meaning "to write."

ascribe (*v.*) əˈskrīb
To attribute something to.

*The recent spate of burglaries was **ascribed** to the spike in unemployment.*

From the Latin meaning "to write in, enter in a list." A more informal way of thinking about this word is "to chalk up," which is somewhat apt since chalk is used for writing.

nondescript (*adj.*) nändəˈskript
Lacking any distinguishing features or qualities.

*The embassy was in a long block of **nondescript** gray buildings and would have been hard to find if not for the flag waving from its entryway.*

The first known use of this word was in the 1680s, derived from the Latin for "not hitherto described." *Unremarkable* and *unexceptional* are two similar words.

inscribe (*v.*) inˈskrīb
To write in or carve on.

*The old couple found the picnic bench where decades earlier they had **inscribed** their names and a heart.*

This comes from Latin, meaning "to write into." *Etch* and *engrave* are two synonyms.

subscribe (*v.*) səbˈskrīb
To believe or attribute validity to.

scribe (*n.*) skrīb
A writer.

conscript (*n.*) kənˈskript
A soldier.

descry (*v.*) diˈskrī
To discern.

ACTIVITY 155

Complete the word for the given definition:

1. con____pt = a soldier

2. in_____e = to write in or carve on

3. sc__b_ = a writer

4. as____e = to attribute

5. su_____e = to believe or attribute validity to

Prefix: *Trans-*

These words incorporate the root *trans-*, meaning "across."

transcribe *(v.)* tranˈskrīb
To turn information—speech, thoughts, etc.—into writing.

*Some of the fastest typists in the world work in the courtroom, where they **transcribe** hours of rapid speech into error-free documents.*

This comes from Latin, meaning "write across." This word can also describe the process of arranging music for an instrument that it was not originally intended for.

transcend *(v.)* tranˈsend
To go beyond the normal, usually in some creative or academic endeavor.

*Even as a teen, her writing **transcended** what professional writers could produce, so few were surprised when she became a staff writer for a respected magazine.*

Comes from the Latin for "climb across." *Eclipse* or *go beyond* are two synonyms for this word.

transgress *(v.)* transˈgres
To stray from what is considered proper or moral behavior.

*He repeatedly **transgressed** the church teachings, yet continued to strive to be a more principled person.*

Another word from Latin, this time meaning "to step across." The noun form of this word is *transgression*.

transverse *(v.)* transˈvərs
To extend across something.

transpose *(v.)* transˈpōz
To swap the position of two things.

transmogrify *(v.)*
transˈmägrəˌfī
To warp.

ACTIVITY 156

Match the word with its meaning:

1. to extend across something _____

2. to betray _____

3. short-lasting _____

4. to warp _____

5. partially transparent _____

6. to go beyond the normal _____

7. to do something not considered proper _____

a. transmogrify

b. transient

c. traduce

d. transcend

e. transgress

f. translucent

g. transverse

Prefix: *Pro-*

This list of words is based on the root *pro-*, meaning "forward."

proponent *(n.)* prəˈpōnənt
A supporter of a cause or way of thinking.

*Though he was an enthusiastic **proponent** of solar panels, his house relied on traditional electricity.*

This is from Latin, meaning "putting forth." The antonym of this word is *opponent*.

protracted *(adj.)* prəˈtraktəd
Lasting longer than expected.

*At three hours running time, the movie felt **protracted**, trying to tie up all the loose plot ends.*

From the Latin for "to draw out." A common word that is a synonym for *protracted* is *prolonged*.

procrastinate *(v.)* rəˈkrastəˌnāt
To delay in carrying out or fulfilling a task.

*Larry always **procrastinated** on school assignments, sometimes staying up until 1:00 a.m. to finish his homework.*

From the Latin for "to put off until tomorrow." A person who procrastinates is called a *procrastinator*.

protuberance *(n.)*
prəˈt(y)o͞ob(ə)rəns
Something that sticks out.

propagate *(v.)* präpəˌgāt
To spread.

provenance *(n.)*
prävənəns
The origin of something.

providential *(adj.)*
prävəˈdenCHəl
Fortunate, happening at just the right time.

prolix *(adj.)* prōˈliks
Talkative.

ACTIVITY 157

Write the word that completes each sentence:

1. He tended to be _____ in public, chatting up total strangers.

2. Since the advent of the Internet, ideas have _____ with greater rapidity than ever before.

Provide the word for the given definition:

3. the origin of something = _____

4. fortunate = _____

5. something that sticks out = _____

6. lasting longer than expected = _____

7. to delay in carrying out a task = _____

Root: *Punct-*

These words are based on the root *punct-*, meaning "pointed."

compunction *(n.)* kəmˈpəNG(k)SHən
A pricking of the conscience, a sense of guilt.

At first he felt elated at finding a $20 bill on the ground, but later he felt **compunction**, *thinking that somebody must be sad that they had lost some money.*

From the Latin "to prick sharply." *Scruples* and *qualms* are two similar words in that they both refer to a sense that one has done or is about to do something wrong.

poignant *(adj.)* poinyənt
Emotionally moving, touching.

The **poignant** *scene in the novel showed the two characters locked in an embrace that they thought would be their last.*

From the Latin "to prick." The root of this word looks different from that found in the other words here because this word, though originally Latin, came from Old French.

punctilio *(n.)* pəNGkˈtilēˌō
A specific point about correct behavior or conduct.

The headmaster chief's **punctilio** *was requiring students to raise their hands before asking a question.*

From Spanish and Italian for "a fine point." This word is related to an earlier word in the book, *punctilious.*

acupuncture *(n.)*
akyəˌpəNGkCHər
The therapeutic use of needles implanted into certain locations on the body.

punctuate *(v.)*
pəNGkCHo͞oˌāt
To add strong emphasis to.

ACTIVITY 158

Provide the word for the given definition:

1. emotionally touching = _____

2. a pricking of the conscience = _____

3. a specific point about correct behavior = _____

4. to add strong emphasis to = _____

Root: *Put-*

These words are based on the root *put-*, meaning "to consider."

disreputable *(adj.)* disˈrepyətəbəl
Not respectable.

*A few **disreputable** establishments at the periphery of town had recently shut down, marking the end of many decades of vice and corruption.*

First used in the 1680s, from Latin for "not reflect upon." An informal synonym is *shady*.

impute *(v.)* imˈpyoōt
To attribute to, ascribe.

*She **imputed** a certain amount of intelligence to those who had graduated from her alma mater, until she met Dexter, who prided himself on his ignorance.*

This comes from the Latin for "to account for." *Ascribe* is a synonym for *impute*.

putative *(adj.)* pyoōtətiv
Supposed, assumed to be.

*He was the **putative** village doctor, though he'd never been to medical school.*

This is from Late Latin, meaning "judge, suppose, thought." A synonym for *putative* that also has the *put-* root is *reputed*.

dispute *(v.)* disˈpyoōt
To argue.

undisputed *(adj.)*
əndiˈspyoōtid
Leaving no room for argument or debate.

deputy *(n.)* depyətē
Someone who answers to the most senior figure in an organization.

ACTIVITY 159

Provide the word for the given definition:

1. leaving no room for debate = _____

2. supposed, in name = _____

3. to attribute to = _____

4. to argue = _____

5. not respectable = _____

Root: *Quisit-*

These words incorporate the root *quisit-*, meaning "to ask."

requisite *(adj.)* rekwəzət
Necessary.

*He didn't have the **requisite** tact to become a diplomat, yet he insisted on entering the foreign service.*

Comes from the Latin, meaning "searched for." This word is also a noun meaning "something that is required."

perquisite *(n.)* pərkwəzit
A benefit from a job (often shortened to *perk*).

*One **perquisite** of working in retail was that he got 30 percent in-store discounts.*

From Medieval Latin, meaning "search thoroughly." This word is commonly confused with *prerequisite* (see below).

prerequisite *(n.)* prēˈrekwəzət
Something that must be fulfilled before something else can happen.

*She hoped to double-major in biology and math but learned that there were so many **prerequisites** to fill, her graduation might delayed by a year.*

From the Latin for "searched for before."

requisition *(n.)*
rekwəˈziSHən
An official document that claims specific goods or property.

inquisition *(n.)*
inkwiˈziSHən
A sustained and often violent questioning.

acquisition *(n.)*
akwəˈziSHən
The attainment of something.

ACTIVITY 160

Provide the word for the given definition:

1. the attainment of something = _____

2. a sustained questioning = _____

3. an official document that claims specific goods = _____

4. something that must be fulfilled before something else can happen = _____

5. a perk = _____

Root: *Rog-*

The following words include the root *rog-*, meaning "to ask."

arrogate *(v.)* arəˌgāt
To take something without justification.

*The new neighbor **arrogated** the land between his fence and his neighbor's fence, using it as a miniature bowling alley.*

Comes from the Latin for "to ask for oneself." This word should not be confused with *abrogate*, which means "to repeal."

surrogate *(n.)* sərəgit
A substitute.

*When professional coaches are sick or cannot attend a game, the assistant manager usually steps in as a **surrogate**.*

From Latin, meaning "put in another's place." Be careful not to use this word for *substitute* in every instance. For example, it would be odd to say that the sick teacher was temporarily replaced by a surrogate teacher.

prerogative *(n.)* priˈrägətiv
A special right that members of a certain group possess.

*The royal family had many **prerogatives**, yet the prince was still thrown in jail for his utter disregard for the law.*

This comes from Medieval Latin, meaning "ask before." This word is similar to *entitlement* and *privilege*.

arrogant *(adj.)* arəgənt
Self-impressed, haughty.

roguish *(adj.)* rōgiSH
Immoral and disreputable but in a way that is charming.

derogate *(v.)* derəˌgāt
To insult.

supererogatory *(adj.)* sōōpəriˈrägəˌtôrē
Beyond what is required.

ACTIVITY 161

Provide the word for the given definition:

1. beyond what is required = _____

2. to insult = _____

3. a special right that members of a certain group possess = _____

4. disreputable in a way that is charming = _____

5. a substitute = _____

6. to take something without justification = _____

Root: *Sequ-*

This list of words is based on the root *sequ-*, meaning "to follow."

subsequent *(adj.)* səbsəkwənt
Coming after.

The original movie was highly praised by critics, whereas all subsequent films in the franchise were described as poor imitators.

This comes from the Latin meaning "following after." This word is often bundled in the phrase "subsequent to."

segue *(v.)* segwā
To transition from one scene to another in an interrupted manner.

The movie segued from one character to the next by having the characters meet each other while walking around in public.

This is from the Latin for "to follow." This word is typically reserved for discussion of music and film.

obsequious *(adj.)* əbˈsēkwēəs
Following someone with slavish obedience.

He acted in an obsequious manner whenever he saw the director, always asking her if she needed a coffee mug filled or another glass of water.

Comes from Latin, meaning "compliant, obedient." On *The Simpsons*, there is an obsequious character named Smithers, who praises his nefarious boss Mr. Burns no matter how vile his behavior.

inconsequential *(adj.)*
inkänsəˈkwenCHəl
Unimportant.

sequester *(v.)* səˈkwestər
To cut off a group from contact with others.

obsequies *(n.)* äbsəkwēz
Funeral rites.

ACTIVITY 162

Write the word that completes each sentence:

1. The first speaker was so charismatic and captivating that all the _____ speakers felt intimidated.

2. Juries are typically _____ during trials that garner national attention.

3. After she found out she'd been accepted to an Ivy League school, the grades she received in her remaining classes seemed _____.

4. Leaders who are surrounded by _____ types become poor at making decisions because nobody ever questions their judgment.

Root: *Ec-*

These words include the root *ec-*, meaning "out of."

eccentric *(adj.)* ik'sentrik
Slightly off, weird.

*She was known for her **eccentric** style of dressing: bright orange skirts, purple boas, and rhinestone cowgirl boots.*

From Medieval Latin, meaning "out of center." This word also describes how much the orbit of one planet around another planet deviates from a perfect circle.

anecdote *(n.)* anik͵dōt
A retelling of something that happened.

*The speaker liked to start his presentations off with a humorous **anecdote,** so the audience would feel relaxed.*

From the Greek for "things published." It's important to remember that an anecdote does not necessarily refer to an event that actually happened to the speaker. These are called "personal anecdotes."

eclectic *(adj.)* i'klektik
A style or idea that comes from a variety of sources.

*His taste in music was **eclectic;** his favorite mix CD contained jazz, hip-hop, classical, and electronic dance music.*

This word comes from Greek, meaning "selective." A simple way to think of this word is *wide-ranging*.

ecstatic *(adj.)* ek'statik
Extremely happy, elated.

appendectomy *(n.)*
apən'dektəmē
The removal of the appendix.

synecdoche *(n.)*
si'nekdəkē
A literary device in which a part of the whole is used to refer to the whole.

ACTIVITY 163

Write the word that completes each sentence:

1. The family's diet was _____, so they enjoyed many different restaurants, including Ethiopian, Indian, Japanese, and Mexican.

2. Upon hearing that she had chosen the winning lotto numbers, the woman was _____.

3. He was so fond of reciting the same personal _____ to strangers that his wife would, in jest, often mouth the words to the story.

4. The _____ scientist—quirky, with wild hair and thick-rimmed glasses—has become a stereotype.

Prefix: *A-* (PART 1)

These words begin with the prefix *a-*, when an "a-" in front of a word doesn't mean "not." It is easy to get carried away with roots, thinking that they apply in all cases. This is clearly not the case, especially when the prefix is the letter "a." Here are a smattering of words beginning with "a" that do not have the prefix "a-", though one might be tempted to apply the root to try to figure out the meaning.

abet *(v.)* əˈbet
To help or assist in wrongdoing.

*A bank guard was incarcerated after having been found guilty of **abetting** the bank robbers.*

Meaning "to urge on" (the *a-* here does not mean "not" but comes from *ad-*, meaning "to"). Remember to use this word only in negative contexts, where something clearly wrong has taken place. Do not use it in place of *help* or *assist*.

ameliorate *(v.)* əˈmēlyəˌrāt
To improve, usually something that is bad.

*Poor living conditions at the periphery were **ameliorated** by donations from charity groups.*

This word comes from French or Medieval Latin, meaning "make better." *Meliorate* means the same thing, so this word can be confusing, especially for those who speak Romance language and assume, mistakenly, that the *a-* means "not."

aficionado *(n.)* əˌfiSH(ē)əˈnädō
A person who is passionate about a specific field or subject.

*Coin-collecting **aficionados**—known as numismatists—are a dying breed since its heyday in the 1970s.*

This word comes from the Spanish for "affectionate." This word is used in Spanish to describe somebody who is devoted to bullfighting.

abut *(v.)* əˈbət
To share a land border with.

abridge *(v.)* əˈbrij
To make shorter.

awry *(adj.)* əˈrī
Not straight.

acolyte *(n.)* akəˌlīt
A follower or disciple.

ACTIVITY 164

Complete the word for the given definition:

1. af_____do = a person passionate about a specific subject

2. a_____e = to make shorter

3. am_____te = to improve something bad

4. a__t = to share a land border with

5. a__t = to assist in a crime

Prefix: *A-* (PART 2)

amnesia *(n.)* amˈnēZHə
The sudden onset of forgetting.

*Soap operas are fond of featuring a character with **amnesia** who suddenly forgets all the dastardly things he or she did.*

This comes from Greek via Modern Latin, meaning "forgetfulness." A person who suffers from amnesia is referred to as an *amnesiac*.

amorphous *(adj.)* əˈmôrfəs
Lacking a discernible shape.

*The oil spill was an **amorphous** black blob in the middle of the lake.*

This word is also from Greek via Modern Latin, meaning "no shape." The word *morph* means "to change from one shape into another."

anomalous *(adj.)* əˈnämələs
Deviating from what is expected.

*Rain in the desert during the summer months is **anomalous**.*

From the Greek for "uneven." *Anomaly* is the noun form.

atypical *(adj.)* āˈtipikəl
Not typical.

amnesty *(n.)* amnistē
Forgiveness, leniency.

atheist *(n.)* āθēˌist
A person who is certain that God or any higher power does not exist.

atrophy *(n.)* atrəfē
Wearing down through the lack of use.

aphasia *(n.)* əˈfāZHə
Inability to speak.

ACTIVITY 165

Write the word that completes each sentence:

1. The teacher found it _____ when the straight-A student forgot her homework three days in a row. (2 possible words)

2. Because the accused was so young, the judge granted _____ and shortened the sentence.

3. Peter broke his arm, and when he removed the cast three months later, _____ had reduced his arm to half its original size.

Provide the word that answers each question:

4. Which word describes a person who does not believe in a higher power? _____

5. Which word means the inability to speak? _____

Root: *Cit-*

These words make use of the root *cit-*, meaning "move."

resuscitate *(v.)* riˈsəsəˌtāt
To bring back to life.

After three years of nothing but losses, there was little left to do to **resuscitate** *the financial firm.*

This comes from the Latin for "raise back." This word is often used literally, especially when CPR is involved, though it can also be used figuratively to describe something inanimate, like a trend or an organization.

cite *(v.)* sīt
To fine.

The motorists were **cited** *for not obeying the traffic laws.*

Comes from Latin via Old French, meaning "to summon." *Cite* can also mean to reference a work, book, or some authority when one is trying to support a claim. This usage becomes more common the more academic the text.

solicitous *(adj.)* səˈlisitəs
Very eager to help, concerned.

The neighbor was **solicitous** *toward the children living next door because she had known them since they were babies.*

From the Latin for "anxiously set in motion." *Solicitude* is the noun form of this word.

recitation *(n.)*
resiˈtāSHən
The act of reading or repeating aloud, often publicly.

unsolicited *(adj.)*
ˌənsəˈlisitid
Not asked for, unwanted.

ACTIVITY 166

Provide the word for the given definition:

1. very eager to help = _____

2. to fine = _____

3. to bring back to life = _____

4. not asked for = _____

Prefix: *Con-* (PART 1)

These words begin with the prefix *con-*, meaning "with."

convivial *(adj.)* kənˈvivēəl
Lively.

*The mood at the baseball game was **convivial** until the home team failed to score.*

This comes from Late Latin, meaning "with life." This word is similar to *vivacious*—lively—however, it typically describes a setting or atmosphere and not a person, the way *vivacious* does.

confluence *(n.)* känˌflo͞oəns
The coming together of two things.

*The European city sat at the **confluence** of the traditional and the modern—gleaming skyscrapers housing financial institutions jostled with centuries-old buildings.*

Another word that comes from Late Latin, this one meaning "flow together." This word can be used to refer to rivers or any fast-moving bodies of water or, in a more literary vein, to describe the coming together of two attributes.

conflate *(v.)* kənˈflāt
To treat or combine two different things as though they were similar.

*It is tempting to **conflate** hard work and success; in reality, a person can work hard and not be successful, and vice versa.*

From the Latin for "blow together." *Conflate* implies that the combining of two things is unintentional, that confusion is involved.

condolence *(n.)*
kənˈdōləns
Regret.

convoke *(v.)* kənˈvōk
To call together.

conclave *(n.)* känˌklāv
A meeting, usually conducted secretly.

consanguinity *(n.)*
känˌsaNGgwinitē
Relatedness through blood.

ACTIVITY 167

Match the word with its meaning:

1. to summon _____

2. lively _____

3. relatedness through blood _____

4. to treat two different things as though they were the same _____

5. the coming together of two different things _____

6. regret _____

a. consanguinity

b. convivial

c. conflate

d. convoke

e. condolence

f. confluence

Prefix: *Con-* (PART 2)

condone *(v.)* kənˈdōn
To not put a stop to something objectionable, thereby implying that it is okay.

The landlord **condoned** *smoking, never saying anything to tenants whose apartments clearly smelled of smoke.*

Comes from Latin, meaning "give altogether." To condone something can be as simple as turning the other way when something bad is happening.

connote *(v.)* kəˈnōt
To mean something beyond the literal definition.

To discriminate simply means to tell the difference between two things; the way the word is generally used, however, **connotes** *targeting a specific group of people.*

From the Latin for "to mark together with." What a word *denotes* is the literal dictionary definition, whereas how the word is used and the associations that go along with it make up what the word *connotes*. The noun form is *connotation*.

conjugal *(adj.)* känjəgəl
Pertaining to the relationship between husband and wife.

The prison allowed two **conjugal** *visits a month.*

Meaning to "tie together" (*-jugal* is derived from a Latin word for "spouse"). *Marital* and *matrimonial* are two common synonyms, whereas *connubial* is a more formal synonym.

congeal *(v.)* kənˈjēl
To turn from liquid to solid.

concentric *(adj.)*
kənˈsentrik
Arranged in overlapping circles.

contiguous *(adj.)*
kənˈtigyo͞os
Bordering, touching.

contumacious *(adj.)*
känt(y)əˈmāSHəs
Stubbornly defiant.

ACTIVITY 168

Provide the word for the given definition:

1. stubbornly defiant = _____

2. pertaining to the relationship between husband and wife = _____

3. bordering = _____

4. to turn from liquid to solid = _____

5. to mean something beyond the literal definition = _____

Prefix: *De-*

These words use the prefix *de-*, meaning "down, completely."

delineate *(v.)* diˈlinēˌāt
To describe in detail.

The psychology teacher spent most of the first class **delineating** *the difference between a psychologist and a psychiatrist.*

From the Latin for "to outline." *Delineate* can also describe the action of marking boundaries on a map.

devolve *(v.)* diˈvälv
To hand off to someone else, delegate.

The president **devolved** *many duties to his cabinet so he could spend more time mending diplomatic ties.*

Again from Latin, meaning "to roll down." This word can also mean "to degenerate" (the opposite of *evolve*). This usage, though, isn't too common.

denude *(v.)* di-ˈn(y)üd
To strip bare, remove any trace of.

The first winter storm swept through the town, leaving the trees **denuded** *of their leaves.*

Meaning "completely bare." This verb will often be used together with "to be," as in "the tree was denuded" vs. "the wind denudes the tree."

descend *(v.)* diˈsend
To move downward.

delimit *(v.)* diˈlimit
To mark the boundaries of.

decipher *(v.)* diˈsīfər
To figure out, discern.

debunk *(v.)* diˈbəNGk
To disprove.

defenestrate *(v.)*
dēˈfenəˌstrāt
To throw someone out of a window (typically used in jest).

decadent *(adj.)* dekədənt
Inclined to disreputable and immoral behavior.

detritus *(n.)* diˈtrītəs
Refuse.

denouement *(n.)*
dānōoˈmän
The falling action after the climax, typically in novels and movies.

ACTIVITY 169

Write the word that completes each sentence:

1. He was skillful at _____ tasks and duties to large groups of people, though he didn't care to do the task himself.

2. Though every story of the Sasquatch has so far been _____, many continue to believe that the latest sighting might be legitimate.

3. The storm left mounds of _____ strewn about the neighborhood.

Unscramble and define:

4. pichered _____

5. dancedte _____

6. meedontune _____

Prefix: *En-* (PART 1)

These words feature the prefix *en-*, meaning "in" or "on."

envisage *(v.)* enˈvizij
To imagine.

*He was so destitute he could not even **envisage** a time when he would own a home.*

This comes from the French for "look in the face of." This word is a more eloquent way of saying *imagine*.

entice *(v.)* enˈtīs
To tempt.

*The brochure made the timeshare seem far more **enticing** than it actually was.*

From a French word meaning "stir up," possibly from Vulgar Latin for "to set on fire." *Lure* and *beguile* are two similar words.

enjoin *(v.)* enˈjoin
To urge someone to do something.

*Her friend's mother **enjoined** her to join the Girl Scouts.*

Comes from Latin for "to join." In a legal context, this word can also mean "prohibit," which makes it confusing.

entourage *(n.)*
äntoōˈräzh
A group that accompanies a celebrity or very important person.

ensue *(v.)* enˈsoō
To follow, in terms of events or actions.

encroach *(v.)* enˈkrōCH
To move in on so as to threaten.

ensconce *(v.)* enˈskäns
To hide.

ACTIVITY 170

Match the word with its meaning:

1. to hide _____

2. to tempt _____

3. to prohibit _____

4. to infringe upon one's boundaries _____

5. to imagine _____

6. to follow, in terms of events _____

a. entice

b. envisage

c. encroach

d. enjoin

e. ensue

f. ensconce

Prefix *En-* (PART 2)

endorse *(v.)* enˈdôrs
To support publicly.

*Some athletes make more money when they **endorse** a product, typically in the form of commercials where they wear a popular shoe brand, than they do from playing the sport itself.*

From the Latin for "on one's back." An endorsement can refer to the backing of somebody for political office or when companies pay lavish sums for athletes to promote their products.

engorge *(v.)* enˈgôrj
To fill with another fluid so that it becomes swollen.

*Ticks become **engorged** with blood after attaching themselves to an animal.*

From the Latin for "into the throat." This word can also mean "to eat too much," as in "to engorge oneself," though this usage is very dated, and "to gorge oneself" is far more common.

enclave *(n.)* enˌklāv
A small area within a larger area.

*There were a few **enclaves** scattered throughout town, where authentic international cuisine abounded.*

From the Latin for "key." This word doesn't just have to describe territory or land but can describe any group that sticks to itself and is isolated from, while being a part of, a larger group.

encompass *(v.)*
enˈkəmpəs
To include or surround entirely.

unencumbered *(adj.)*
ənenˈkəmbərd
Not weighed down by obligations.

enthrall *(v.)* enˈθrôl
To hold spellbound.

encomium *(n.)*
enˈkōmēəm
Speech that highly praises.

ACTIVITY 171

Match the word with its meaning:

1. to surround entirely _____   a. endorse

2. to hold spellbound _____   b. enthrall

3. high praise _____   c. encomium

4. to swell with liquid _____   d. engorge

5. to support publicly _____   e. enclave

6. a small area within a larger area _____   f. encompass

Root: *E-*

These words use the root *e-*, meaning "out of" or "from."

enormity *(n.)* iˈnôrmitē
Wickedness.

*The **enormity** of twentieth-century dictators will hopefully serve as a check on those who wield power in this century.*

From the Latin for "out of the pattern." This word is often thought to mean "enormousness," though the words are very different. Nonetheless, this erroneous usage is gaining ground and might soon be accepted.

ineluctable *(adj.)* iniˈləktəbəl
Unavoidable.

*Since he had failed to appear in court twice for a spate of speeding tickets, an even heftier fine was **ineluctable**.*

From the Latin for "not struggle out." *Inescapable* and *inevitable* are two synonyms.

evocative *(adj.)* iˈväkətiv
Causing one to have a vivid recollection of something.

*Her writing was so **evocative** of the places she had visited that it was as though the reader were traipsing through the same foreign lands.*

This word comes from the Latin for "summoning forth." The verb form is *evoke*.

enunciate *(v.)* iˈnənsēˌāt
To pronounce very clearly.

elocution *(n.)*
eləˈkyo͞oSHən
The proper way of speaking and pronouncing.

emolument *(n.)*
iˈmälyəmənt
Payment given for work done.

ACTIVITY 172

Write the word that completes each sentence:

1. The _____ of the crime carried with it a life sentence.

2. She asked the teacher to repeat himself and to _____ each syllable.

3. The hurricane was _____, bearing down upon the small island with catastrophic winds.

Give the word for each definition:

4. the proper way of speaking = _____

5. causing one to have a vivid recollection = _____

Root: *Fact-*

The words below contain the root *fact-*, meaning "made."

factoid *(n.)* fak ̤toid
A tidbit of inaccurate information that has been repeated so often it is accepted as true.

*The campaign speech contained numerous questionable **factoids** without providing reliable sources for them.*

This word comes from *fact* plus the suffix *-oid*, which means "having the appearance of." *Factoid* can carry a slightly negative connotation, implying that whatever the factoid is describing is somewhat trivial.

factotum *(n.)* fakˈtōtəm
A person who does odd jobs.

*Jenny was the office's **factotum**, able to take care of anything from maintenance issues to legal matters.*

From the Latin for "do everything." *Jack-of-all-trades* is a more common way of saying this word (though *factotum* is more gender neutral).

olfactory *(adj.)* älˈfakt(ə)rē
Relating to the sense of smell.

*His severe head cold had diminished his **olfactory** sense to the point that he couldn't discriminate between chicken soup and tomato soup.*

This is from the Latin for "smell."

artifact *(n.)* ärtə ̤fakt
A physical object made by a person.

putrefaction *(n.)*
pyo͞otrəˈfakSHən
The decay and rotting of flesh.

factious *(adj.)* fakSHəs
Marked by inner conflict.

factitious *(adj.)*
fakˈtiSHəs
Fictional, not real.

ACTIVITY 173

Match the word with its meaning:

1. fictional _____

2. the process of rotting _____

3. a human-made object of historical interest _____

4. relating to smell _____

5. Jack-of-all-trades _____

6. a tidbit of inaccurate information _____

a. factotum

b. factoid

c. olfactory

d. putrefaction

e. artifact

f. factitious

Root: *Fic-*

These words build upon the root *fic-*, meaning "to do."

prolific *(adj.)* prəˈlifik
Creating something in abundance.

*Haydn was a **prolific** composer, writing over 100 symphonies in his lifetime.*

From the Latin for "offspring." This word was traditionally used to describe a woman who bore many offspring, though this usage has become outdated. Today, *prolific* is used more commonly to describe creative output (see example sentence).

ramification *(n.)* raməfəˈkāSHən
A consequence, typically an unwanted one.

*The municipal board had not thought through the **ramifications** of doubling the price of utilities: Soon there was a major shortage of renters.*

From the French for "to form branches." This word is similar to *aftermath*, though the latter tends to imply something with very serious consequences.

pontificate *(v.)* pänˈtifiˌkāt
To speak pompously and in a highly opinionated manner.

*Matt didn't know much, but sometimes it was hard to tell by the way he **pontificated**.*

From the Latin *pontifex* (*pontiff* is another name for the pope). "To speak dogmatically" is another way of thinking about this word.

fortification *(n.)*
fôrtəˌfəˈkāSHən
A strong defense.

edifice *(n.)* ˈedəfis
A building.

ratification *(n.)*
ratəfəˈkāSHən
The process by which a treaty is made officially valid.

edification *(n.)*
edəfiˈkāSHən
The process by which someone is improved on a deep level.

ACTIVITY 174

Match the word with its meaning:

1. a strong defense _____

2. confirmation of a treaty _____

3. to improve on a deeper level _____

4. unforeseen consequence _____

5. building _____

6. to speak pompously _____

a. edify

b. edifice

c. ramification

d. pontificate

e. ratification

f. fortification

Root: *Gen-*

The words below include the root *gen-*, meaning "born."

progeny *(n.)* prä'jənē
One's offspring.

His **progeny**—*all three children and seven grandchildren—went on to attend college.*

From the Latin for "beget," which means to bring a child into the world. The word *progenitor*, which shares the same root, means "parent."

indigenous *(adj.)* in'dijənəs
Native to a specific country.

Many **indigenous** *plants had succumbed to drought, so they brought in non-native species that could survive on less rainfall.*

This comes from the Latin for "native." This word should not be confused with *indignant* (meaning "angry") or *indigent* (meaning "poor").

carcinogenic *(adj.)* kärsənə'jenik
Cancer-causing.

After the factory fire, the atmosphere was deemed **carcinogenic,** *and residents were advised to stay indoors.*

From the Latin for "cancer." *Carcinogen* is the noun form of this word.

genesis *(n.)* 'jenəsis
Beginning, origin.

genealogy *(n.)* jēnē'äləjē
One's family tree.

genocide *(n.)* jenə,sīd
The killing of all the people of a certain group.

endogenous *(adj.)*
en'däjənəs
Originating internally.

ACTIVITY 175

Unscramble and define:

1. encodige _____

2. singese _____

3. dousingeni _____

Write the word that completes each sentence:

4. Jack traced his _____ back six generations.

5. Many things in our environment are _____ if we are exposed to them enough.

Suffix: *-Gress*

These words contain the suffix *-gress*, meaning "step."

regress *(v.)* ri'gres
To return to a former, inferior state.

*Without his aunt to check his homework every day, Harold **regressed** to his old habit of staying up until midnight watching TV.*

This is from Latin, meaning "walk back." The noun form of this word is *regression*.

digress *(v.)* dī'gres
To stray from the main topic.

*The professor **digressed** from the main topic and soon the students lost interest.*

Comes from Latin, meaning "walk away." *Digression* is the noun form of this word.

progressive *(adj.)* prə'gresiv
Having liberal views or views that promote innovative ideas.

*The political divide in that country is marked by conservatives, who want to keep things the way they are, and **progressives**, who are constantly looking for new approaches.*

This possibly comes from the French for "gone forward." Politically speaking, progressives are on the other side of the spectrum from conservatives.

congress *(n.)* käNGgrəs
The coming together of political groups.

ingress *(n.)* in͵gres
Entrance.

egress *(n.)* ē͵gres
Exit.

ACTIVITY 176

Match the word with its definition:

1. exit _____
2. entrance _____
3. the coming together of political groups _____
4. to stray from the main topic _____
5. to return to a former state _____

a. digress
b. egress
c. congress
d. regress
e. ingress

Root: *-Graph*

This list of words contains the root *-graph*, meaning "to write."

calligraphy *(n.)* kəˈligrəfē
The art of decorative writing.

*Though some believe that the Internet has made **calligraphy** a dying art, there are small pockets of enthusiasts who keep the tradition alive.*

This comes from Greek, meaning "beautiful writing." Calligraphy got the spotlight when Steve Jobs revealed that one of the most important classes he ever took was a calligraphy class because it taught him the importance of design.

topography *(n.)* təˈpägrəfē
The description of the physical features of the landscape.

*On the second day of the hike, the **topography** had changed markedly, the rolling foothills giving way to jagged peaks.*

This is from Greek via Late Latin, meaning "place writing." Topographical maps show the altitudes of the land they cover.

demographics *(n.)* deməˈgrafiks
The study of the components of a population.

*The **demographics** of the city had changed in the last 50 years, with the influx of young immigrants.*

Meaning "people writing," the first known use of this word was in the late 1960s. A *demographer* is one who studies *demographics*.

graphite *(n.)* graˌfīt
A mineral that is used for the lead of pencils.

cartography *(n.)* kärˈtägrəfē
The writing of maps, mapmaking.

bibliography *(n.)* biblēˈägrəfē
A list of books, typically in an appendix.

choreography *(n.)* kôrēˈägrəfē
The creation and arrangement of dance movements.

graphologist *(n.)* graˈfäləjist
A person who studies handwriting.

ACTIVITY 177

Match the word with its meaning:

1. dance composition _____

2. pencil lead _____

3. list of books _____

4. one who studies handwriting _____

5. map making _____

6. study of population groups _____

a. cartography

b. bibliography

c. graphite

d. choreography

e. demographics

f. graphologist

Root: *Ig-*

The following words utilize the root *ig-*, meaning "to act or do."

ambiguous *(adj.)* ambiˈgyo͞owəs
Vague because of having more than one possible interpretation.

*When his mother told Fred to leave his lunchbox by the door, he found the instructions **ambiguous** because the house had a front door and a back door.*

From the Latin for "doubtful." *Ambiguity* is the noun form of this word.

mitigate *(v.)* mitəˌgāt
To lessen the severity.

*Hoping to **mitigate** the disappointment of his 2.1 GPA, Hank told his parents that he had made the basketball team.*

From the Latin for "softened." Do not confuse *mitigate* with *militate*, which means "to prevent something from happening" (and is used with the preposition "against").

castigate *(v.)* kastəˌgāt
To criticize harshly.

*He was **castigated** for not letting his boss know that he would be returning from vacation four days later than expected.*

This is from the Latin for "reprove," which is another way of saying scolding. *Castigate* is typically only used in formal contexts.

navigate *(v.)* naviˌgāt
To guide a vehicle or to travel over a specific course.

exigent *(adj.)* eksijənt
Urgent.

unmitigated *(adj.)* ənˈmitəˌgātid
Absolute, not lessened (typically describes a negative word).

ACTIVITY 178

Write the word that completes each sentence:

1. The minivan was unable to _____ around the snowdrift.

2. It is _____ that the building be evacuated immediately.

3. The new hire just out of college had the _____ nerve to tell his boss how to run the business.

Provide the word for the given definition:

4. vague = _____

5. to lessen the severity of = _____

6. to criticize harshly = _____

Root: *Pend-*

The following words are based on the root *pend-*, meaning "to hang."

appendix *(n.)* əˈpendiks
Something that comes at the end of a book describing additional topics relevant to the book.

*The **appendix** to the Spanish language book contained conjugations for the 500 most common verbs.*

From the Latin for "hang upon." Another definition of *appendix* is "a small sac that has no known function in humans but in some animals is used to process cellulose."

compendious *(adj.)* kəmˈpendēəs
Comprehensive but concise.

*Her survey of Roman history is **compendious**, touching all the main parts without going into unnecessary detail.*

This is from the Latin for "brief and advantageous." The related word *compendium* describes a large book that contains comprehensive information on a certain subject.

impending *(adj.)* imˈpendiNG
About to happen.

*With an **impending** deadline, Tiffany worked efficiently.*

This word also comes from Latin, meaning "hanging." Another way of saying this is *looming*.

appendage *(n.)* əˈpendij
Something that is a part of a larger thing.

pending *(adj.)* pendiNG
Describing an issue that is awaiting a decision so it can be settled.

expenditure *(n.)* ikˈspendiCHər
The spending of money.

ACTIVITY 179

Provide the word for the given definition:

1. section found at the back of a book = _____

2. about to happen = _____

3. describes a decision that is yet to be settled = _____

4. describes something both comprehensive and concise = _____

5. the payment of something = _____

Root: *Reg-*

These words include the root *reg-*, meaning "rule."

regicide *(n.)* rejə͵sīd
The killing of a king or queen.

Regicide is common in the works of Shakespeare.

From the Latin for "royal killing." *The Lion King* and *Hamlet* (on which the movie is partially based) begin with a memorable regicide.

regalia *(n.)* riˈgālyə
The symbols of royalty, such as the crown.

*The **regalia** of the Romanov empire—from Fabergé eggs to a formidable scepter—were on display at the local museum.*

Comes from Latin, meaning "royal privileges."

regal *(adj.)* rēgəl
Royal in manner, like a king.

regent *(n.)* rējənt
A person who rules a country in the absence of the king or queen.

regiment *(n.)* ˈrejəmənt
The largest unit in an army that is broken down into smaller units.

regnant *(adj.)* regnənt
Ruling, dominant.

ACTIVITY 180

Provide the word for the given definition:

1. ruling = _____

2. the largest unit in an army = _____

3. the killing of a king or queen = _____

4. the symbols of royalty = _____

5. a person who rules in the absence of the king or queen = _____

6. royal in manner = _____

Words Beginning with A

The remaining lessons will address words beginning with a specific letter of the alphabet, starting with A and working alphabetically through most of the letters. These words didn't happen to fall into one of the groupings in the previous lessons, but they are important words to know.

ascertain *(v.)* asərˈtān
To determine something.

Scientists ascertained that the asteroid would miss Earth by tens of thousands of miles.

From the Latin for "settled." A simple synonym for this word is "figure out."

antiquated *(adj.)* antiˌkwātid
Old-fashioned.

Each generation thinks the previous generation's dance moves are antiquated.

This is from the Latin for "to make old." *Antiquarian*, a similar-looking word, refers to someone who collects antiques.

accretion *(n.)* əˈkrēSHən
The buildup of something.

The accretion of debris at the river mouth caused a blockage, and water began to trickle where before it had flowed.

Comes from the Latin for "to become larger." The word *accrue*, which means "to build up over time," is related to accretion.

adulate *(v.)* ajəˌlāt
To praise to the point of worship.

admonish *(v.)* ədˈmäniSH
To warn and criticize at the same time.

agrarian *(adj.)*
əˈgre(ə)rēən
Relating to the countryside, rural.

ailment *(n.)* ālmənt
Illness.

ACTIVITY 181

Write the word that completes each sentence:

1. She _____ her children not to leave the house once it got dark.

2. An _____ revolution took place, whereby all the farmers refused to sell their crops.

3. Today, CEOs are often _____ the way pop stars are.

4. At first it was difficult for detectives to _____ the motive for the crime.

5. Just as stagecoaches have become_____, one day so too will automobiles.

Words Beginning with B

banter *(n.)* bantər
Light teasing.

*Though to an outsider Tyler's friends' words sounded hostile, Tyler knew it was mere **banter**.*

The origin of this word is not known. *Repartee* and *raillery* are somewhat common words similar to *banter*.

bedlam *(n.)* bedləm
Utter chaos.

***Bedlam** broke out in the lecture hall when a giant rat scurried across the front of the room.*

This word comes from the name of the hospital for the insane. *Pandemonium* is a synonym.

belie *(v.)* biˈlī
To show to be false, contradict.

*Her calm demeanor **belied** the anger raging inside her.*

From Old English for "to lie." "To be at odds with" is another way of thinking of this word.

bemoan *(v.)* biˈmōn
To lament, express sorrow over.

beguile *(v.)* biˈgīl
To deceive in a charming way.

berate *(v.)* biˈrāt
To criticize at length.

betrothed *(n.)* bəˈtrōθt
One to be married.

ACTIVITY 182

Match the word with its meaning:

1. to lamet _____

2. to criticize at length _____

3. to deceptively charm _____

4. be at odds with _____

5. hysteria _____

6. light teasing _____

a. beguile

b. belie

c. bedlam

d. berate

e. bemoan

f. banter

Words Beginning with C

caustic *(adj.)* kôstik
Very harsh.

*His words were so **caustic**, so painful to hear, that she decided to no longer be friends with him.*

From the Greek "to burn." The definition and example sentence use the word figuratively. Literally, this word describes chemicals that burn.

collude *(v.)* kəˈloōd
To conspire.

*Documents revealed that different governmental agencies had **colluded**.*

This word is from the Latin for "have a secret agreement." The noun form of this word, *collusion*, is also common.

cantankerous *(adj.)* kanˈtaNGkərəs
Ill-tempered.

*The later it got the more **cantankerous** Uncle Phil became, berating his nephews for no reason at all.*

From an Anglo-Irish word made up of *cankerous* and *rancorous*. *Irascible* and *choleric* are two other ways of thinking about this word, whereas *grumpy* is a more straightforward description.

clamber *(v.)* klambər
To climb up something, usually in an awkward manner.

catatonic *(adj.)* kadəˈtänik
Describing a mental state where someone is completely unresponsive.

carouse *(v.)* kəˈrouz
To go around partying.

commiserate *(v.)*
kəˈmizəˌrāt
To sympathize.

ACTIVITY 183

Write the word that completes each sentence:

1. Both Tommy and Becky had dropped their ice cream cones, so they _____ over hot cocoa.

2. The intrepid father made his way into the child's fun house, daftly _____ up the net walls.

3. After the accident, she remained _____ for days before returning to full health.

Provide the definition:

4. carouse = _____

5. cantankerous = _____

6. collude = _____

Words Beginning with D

divulge *(v.)* diˈvəlj
To reveal (typically something that should remain hidden).

*Once the magician **divulged** all of his secrets, the public no longer found his act engaging.*

From the Latin for to "publish widely." *Disclose* is a synonym for *divulge*.

deign *(v.)* dān
To do something one thinks is below them, to stoop.

*She did not even **deign** to reply to the man's impertinent comment.*

This comes from the Latin for "to deem worthy." This word is often used with the word *not* (as in the sample sentence).

disdain *(n.)* disˈdān
Intense dislike.

*His **disdain** for loud public spaces was known to all of his friends, who usually met with him at a quiet café.*

Also from Latin, meaning "not considering worthy." *Contempt* is a good synonym to know.

demonstrative *(adj.)*
diˈmänstrətiv
Emotionally expressive.

delirious *(adj.)*
diˈli(ə)rēəs
In a wild state, where one cannot tell the difference between what is real and what is in one's mind.

dismay *(n.)* disˈmā
Sudden loss of courage, sudden disappointment.

dilapidated *(adj.)*
diˈlapiˌdātd
Run-down, usually describing a structure or building.

disparage *(v.)* diˈsparij
To insult.

ACTIVITY 184

Match the word with its meaning:

1. to spill the beans _____

2. run-down _____

3. sudden disappointment _____

4. to put down _____

5. emotionally expressive _____

6. to do something one considers below one's dignity _____

7. intense hate _____

a. dilapidated

b. deign

c. disdain

d. disparage

e. divulge

f. dismay

g. demonstrative

Words Beginning with E

eschew *(v.)* esˈchoo
To shun, avoid using.

*She **eschewed** all forms of merrymaking while training for the triathlon.*

From the German for "to shun." *Abstain* is an important synonym to know.

eradicate *(v.)* iˈradiˌkāt
To wipe out any trace of, kill completely.

*Though the exterminators had promised to **eradicate** the cockroaches in the Millers' home, as soon as the family returned, a giant one scuttled across the kitchen floor.*

Comes from the Latin "to pull up from the roots." A fancy synonym, rarely seen outside of standardized tests, is *extirpate*.

elegant *(adj.)* eləgənt
Graceful, effective yet straightforward.

*Though the teacher showed a solution to a difficult math question, a discerning pupil arrived at an even more **elegant** explanation.*

This is from the Latin for "to choose" or "select." This definition of the word is not too common but is useful to know in college when taking science courses or any course that discusses experiments.

entertain *(v.)* entərˈtān
To consider.

evident *(adj.)* evədənt
Obvious, easily seen.

espouse *(v.)* iˈspouz
To support, typically a belief or an idea.

endow *(v.)* enˈdou
To give ability to.

ACTIVITY 185

Write the word that completes each sentence:

1. He did not _____ ideas that did not rest on strong scientific evidence.

2. She was _____ with a kind, generous spirit.

3. Her musical talent was _____ from a young age, when she was able to play sonatas from memory.

4. The family of four would not even _____ the notion of living in an apartment.

5. The gardener was unable to _____ the weeds and they grew back the following year.

Words Beginning with F

finagle (*v.*) fəˈnāgəl
To get something through trickery.

*Charming and witty, Patty was usually able to **finagle** free drink refills at the burger joint.*

This word is of an uncertain origin but likely popped up in the United States around 100 years ago. *Finagle* is typically used informally.

foist (*v.*) foist
To force something upon someone.

*Chuck **foisted** his old rock albums on his kids, who invariably put them aside without ever listening to them.*

This word comes from a Dutch dialect. This word is usually embedded in the phrase "to foist someone/something on" e.g., his parents constantly foisted job ads on him.

festoon (*v.*) fesˈto͞on
To decorate a place, usually with garlands.

*To spruce up his apartment for the housewarming, Oliver **festooned** it with black and red garlands, in honor of his love of checkers.*

From the Italian for "feast." *Festoon*, loosely speaking, can also mean "to adorn with any decorations, not necessarily rope-like."

fritter (*v.*) fritər
To waste (typically time or resources).

feral (*adj.*) ferəl
Wild.

filigree (*n.*) filəˌgrē
Fanciful decoration around the edges.

fickle (*adj.*) fikəl
Constantly changing one's mind.

ACTIVITY 186

Write the word that completes each sentence:

1. The cat was _____, one moment lavishing attention on a guest and the next moment hissing at them.

2. The dog was _____ despite the best efforts of the Robertsons to tame it.

3. Each year college students bemoan that 10-pound textbooks are _____ on them.

Define the word:

4. fritter _____

5. filigree _____

6. festoon _____

Words Beginning with G

germane *(adj.)* jərˈmān
Relevant to whatever is being discussed.

Questions not germane to the topic were removed from the online Q&A session, since the speaker was given only 20 minutes to answer.

This word originally meant "German," but the way it is used today can be traced back to Shakespeare's *Hamlet.* A synonym for *germane* is *pertinent.*

garner *(v.)* gärnər
To gather.

Despite his efforts to appeal to the entire electorate, the governor was unable to garner support from the working class.

From the Latin for "granary." A synonym for this word is *collect.*

gentrification *(n.)* jentrəfiˈkāSHən
The process of turning a run-down area into a hip area.

Once an area avoided by the middle class and wealthy, the downtown had undergone gentrification and was now a mecca of art galleries and Parisian-style cafes.

From an Anglo–Irish word describing those who were enchanted. The *gentry* are a group from a high social class.

gripe *(v.)* grīp
To complain persistently.

glom *(v.)* glam
To grab on to.

glum *(adj.)* gləm
Depressed, sullen.

grovel *(v.)* grävəl
To beg pathetically when asking for forgiveness.

ACTIVITY 187

Match the word with its meaning:

1. renovation of a downtrodden area _____

2. blue _____

3. to beg obsequiously _____

4. to grab on to _____

5. to gather _____

6. relevant to _____

7. to complain constantly _____

a. grovel

b. garner

c. glum

d. gripe

e. germane

f. gentrification

g. glom

Words Beginning with H

heretic *(n.)* herətik
A person who believes in something that is at odds with the prevailing belief.

*Many tea enthusiasts claim that one should always add milk after steeping teabags, but Jonathan is a **heretic**, believing that the teabags should be steeped in boiling milk.*

From the Greek for "to choose." This word was traditionally used to describe those who went against church teachings but now has a broader application.

hegemony *(n.)* həˈjemənē
Dominance of one nation over another or one group over another.

*After defeating the Spanish Armada in 1588, Great Britain gained **hegemony** of the Atlantic and retained it for centuries to come.*

This comes from the Greek for "leader." *Dominance* is a synonym for *hegemony*.

husbandry *(n.)* həzbəndrē
The careful management of resources.

__Husbandry__ was essential during the two-week desert trek; the nomads carefully measured, down to the nearest ounce, the amount of water consumed.

This word is related to "husband," in the now-obsolete sense of "peasant farmer." *Animal husbandry* refers to the careful management of livestock.

haven *(n.)* hāvən
A safe place, refuge.

hallow *(v.)* halo
To make sacred.

hirsute *(adj.)* hər͵sōot
Hairy.

harry *(v.)* ˈherē, ˈharē
To harass incessantly.

ACTIVITY 188

Match the word with its meaning:

1. management of resources _____

2. safe place _____

3. persistently harass _____

4. sacred _____

5. dominance _____

6. one who does not subscribe to prevailing belief _____

7. hairy _____

a. hirsute

b. heretic

c. hegemony

d. hallowed

e. harry

f. haven

g. husbandry

Words Beginning with I

inveterate (*adj.*) inˈvetərit
Describing a deeply ingrained habit.

*Wilson was an **inveterate** stock trader and couldn't imagine a morning without trading.*

From the Latin for "made old." This word is typically used to describe a bad habit.

inoculate (*v.*) iˈnäkyəˌlāt
To protect against disease by giving a vaccine to.

*Before babies can be released from the hospital, they must be **inoculated**.*

Comes from the Latin for "into eye." The noun form of the word is *inoculation*.

impervious (*adj.*) imˈpərvēəs
Unaffected by, immune to.

*While the wrestler feigned to be **impervious** to pain, the morning after every bout, he'd grimace when getting out of bed.*

From the Latin for "not passing through." This word can also describe something physical in which liquid cannot pass through, such as a raincoat. When used in this way, *impermeable* is a good synonym to know.

itinerary (*n.*) īˈtinəˌrerē
A breakdown or description of one's travel plans.

idiom (*n.*) idēəm
A saying that is particular to a language.

intuitive (*adj.*)
inˈt(y)o̅o̅itiv
Not based on rational assessment, from the gut.

imprint (*v.*) imˈprint
To leave a lasting impression.

impetus (*n.*) impitəs
Motivation.

ACTIVITY 189

Write the word that completes each sentence:

1. He lacked any _____ and felt himself drifting through life.

2. Her experience with the Peace Corps left a lifelong _____.

3. She trusted his _____, even though she couldn't say exactly why he knew something bad was going to happen.

4. "Every dog has its day" is an example of an _____.

5. She was _____ to negative criticism, able to create great work no matter what her critics said.

Words Beginning with L

lithe *(adj.)* līᵺ
Flexible.

*She was never **lithe**, finding activities like ballet and gymnastics difficult.*

From the German for "soft" and "gentle." *Graceful* and *supple* are two good synonyms to know.

livid *(adj.)* livid
Extremely angry.

*After receiving two parking tickets for the same infraction, Liz became **livid**.*

Comes from the French for "bluish." There are many words in English that are synonyms for *livid*, among them *fuming*, *furious*, *infuriated*, *irate*, and *incensed*.

languorous *(adj.)* laNGərəs
Pleasantly tired, lethargic.

*For Rick, vacations meant taxing day hikes; his wife, though, couldn't be more different, enjoying **languorous** afternoons poolside.*

This word comes from the Latin for "loose, lax." The noun form of this word is *languor*.

leery *(adj.)* li(ə)rē
Suspicious of real dangers.

lull *(n.)* ləl
A break in the action, downtime.

liable *(adj.)* lī(ə)bəl
Accountable for something.

lumber *(v.)* ləmbər
To move clumsily.

ACTIVITY 190

Match the word with its meaning:

1. to move clumsily _____

2. suspicious _____

3. pleasantly tired _____

4. a momentary pause in the action _____

5. very angry _____

6. flexible _____

a. lull

b. leery

c. lumber

d. lithe

e. languorous

f. livid

Words Beginning with M

mirth *(n.)* mərTH
Laughter and merriment.

There was mirth in the air at the Christmas party, with eggnog and gifts flowing freely.

From the German for "merry." The adjective form of this word is *mirthful*.

mettle *(n.)* metl
The ability to endure despite tough circumstances.

During the days in which the soldiers were in the trenches, they had to keep their mettle, at the risk of losing their minds.

Despite the different spelling, this word is related to *metal*. The adjective *mettlesome* should not be confused with the word *meddlesome*, which means "to be eager to learn about affairs that do not directly concern oneself."

myopic *(adj.)* mīˈäpik
Shortsighted or lacking foresight.

The firm was myopic, focusing mostly on the quarter gains, and did not plan adequately for the upcoming year.

From the Greek for "to shut the eye." This word can also describe someone who is literally nearsighted and needs glasses.

maim *(v.)* mām
To cause permanent injury to.

meager *(adj.)* mēgər
Pathetically small in amount.

meander *(v.)* mēˈandər
To move indirectly.

mull *(v.)* məl
To consider.

ACTIVITY 191

Unscramble and define:

1. luml _____

2. amender _____

3. ammi _____

4. compyi _____

5. rithm _____

Words Beginning with N

negligible *(adj.)* neglijəbəl
Having little to no effect, insignificant.

*Though the rain was welcome by the drought-stricken region, the amount proved **negligible**, in some places less than a quarter inch.*

From the French for "to neglect." This word should not be confused with *negligent*, which means not properly doing what one has been tasked to do.

nadir *(n.)* nādər
Lowest point.

*Though she went on to become a successful CEO, she remembered her **nadir** distinctly, when she had a weekend gig as "Molly the Clown."*

The word comes from the Arabic for "lowest point." This word isn't typically used to describe a physical lowest point (like Death Valley) but rather the point in one's life or career where one is at the bottom-most point.

noisome *(adj.)* noisəm
Extremely foul smelling.

*The **noisome** vapors emanating from the factory worried those in town.*

This word is related to the word "annoy." *Noisome* does not have anything to do with noise.

nimble *(adj.)* nimbəl
Agile, quick.

nary *(adj.)* ne(ə)rē
Not any.

natter *(v.)* natər
To chatter.

natty *(adj.)* natē
Wearing nice, fashionable clothes.

ACTIVITY 192

Write the word that completes each sentence:

1. She had a _____ mind, able to dissect her opponent's argument quickly and offer an eloquent rebuttal.

2. The teacher admonished the students in the back not to _____ while he spoke.

3. There was _____ a drop of water left in their canisters after the nine-hour hike.

Provide the word for the given definition:

4. extremely foul smelling = _____

5. lowest point = _____

6. insignificant = _____

Words Beginning with O

ominous *(adj.)* ämənəs
Threatening, menacing.

*Upon seeing the **ominous** rainclouds on the horizon, the children returned indoors.*

From the Latin for "omen" or "sign." While an *omen* can be a sign prophesizing something either good or bad, *ominous* refers only to something bad.

omnipotent *(adj.)* ämˈnipətənt
All-powerful.

*On the baseball diamond, Babe Ruth seemed **omnipotent**, able to send the ball flying over the fences with a single swat of his bat.*

This comes from the Latin for "all-powerful." This word should not be confused with *omniscient*, which means "all-knowing."

ossify *(v.)* äsəˌfī
To harden, become rigid and inflexible.

*Once an agile company, able to adapt to the market, it had **ossified** into one full of managers concerned only with getting promoted.*

From the Latin for "bone." The definition provided above is figurative. *Ossify* can also refer to the physical process by which tissue becomes bony.

opine *(v.)* ōˈpīn
To express an opinion.

oeuvre *(n.)* œvrə
The *oe* is pronounced like the "u" in *full*.
The complete work of an author, musician, or artist.

ornery *(adj.)* ôrn(ə)rē
Mean-spirited, cantankerous.

onerous *(adj.)* ōnərəs
Burdensome.

ACTIVITY 193

Match the word with its meaning:

1. to express an opinion _____
2. to harden, become rigid _____
3. all-powerful _____
4. threatening _____
5. complete body of work _____
6. cantankerous _____
7. burdensome _____

a. ornery
b. onerous
c. opine
d. omnipotent
e. oeuvre
f. ominous
g. ossify

Words Beginning with P

perpetuate *(v.)* pərˈpeCHo͞oˌāt
To make something last indefinitely.

*The Internet has a way of **perpetuating** untruths—when we continue to see the same "facts" online, we begin to think them true.*

This word is from the Latin for "made permanent." The adjective form of the word—*perpetual*—is just as common, if not more common.

prevaricate *(v.)* priˈvariˌkāt
To deviate from the truth, to lie.

*When Greg caught his wife hiding his Christmas present in their closet, she began to **prevaricate**, saying the box was just filled with old stuff.*

From the Latin for "to walk crookedly." Synonyms for *prevaricate* are *equivocate* and *lie*. *Prevaricate* is the least accusatory of the terms.

penchant *(n.)* penCHənt
A strong liking or fondness for something; an inclination.

*He had a **penchant** for collecting stuff from bygone generations.*

This comes from the French for "leaning." *Propensity* and *proclivity* are two synonyms for *penchant*.

peddle *(v.)* pedl
To sell, hawk.

pander *(v.)* pandər
To indulge the baser instincts of.

preempt *(v.)* prēˈempt
To take or do before someone else can.

pilfer *(v.)* pilfər
To steal.

ACTIVITY 194

Complete the word for the given definition:

1. pil_____ = to steal

2. pre_____ = to take or do before someone else can

3. pan_____ = to indulge the baser instincts of

4. pen_____ = fondness

5. pre_____ = to deviate from the truth

6. ped_____ = to sell

7. per_____ = to make something last indefinitely

Words Beginning with Q

quagmire *(n.)* kwag͵mīr
A situation difficult to get out of or escape.

After he had double-booked two important interviews, he found himself in a **quagmire**.

A *quag* is swampy ground, and a *mire* is also swampy ground. Put them together and you get a very swampy ground, from which it can be difficult to extract one's foot. Former Secretary of Defense Donald Rumsfeld famously claimed that Iraq was not becoming a quagmire, though the war had no end in sight.

quixotic *(adj.)* kwikˈsätik
Wildly impractical.

The governor claimed to have many great ideas, but they were so **quixotic** *that even his supporters knew there was no way he could pull them off.*

This word comes from the literary character Don Quixote, known for his delusional schemes and loose grip on reality. *Quixotic* is typically used in the context of a project or venture. While you can use *quixotic* to describe a person, typically *impractical* or *idealistic* will do.

quisling *(n.)* kwizling
A traitor, specially one who is in league with an enemy.

When the firm was bought and new management took over, most knew it was time to find another job, save for a few **quislings** *who had begun getting chummy with the new bosses.*

This word came into use after World War II. Vidkun Quisling was a Norwegian major in the army whom Germany installed as the leader of Norway between 1940 and 1945.

quip *(v.)* kwip
To make a clever comment.

quandary *(n.)*
kwänd(ə)rē
A difficult situation in which you don't know what to do.

quizzical *(adj.)* kwizəkəl
Confused, puzzled.

querulous *(adj.)*
kwer(y)ələs
Complaining constantly.

ACTIVITY 195

Match the word with its meaning:

1. collaborator with the enemy _____
2. puzzled _____
3. dilemma _____
4. to make a witty comment _____
5. complaining _____
6. wildly idealistic _____

a. quixotic
b. quisling
c. quizzical
d. quip
e. quandary
f. querulous

Words Beginning with R

refine *(v.)* riˈfīn
To make more pure, to remove impurities from.

*She was able to **refine** her dissertation before presenting it before the committee.*

Meaning "finish again," from the French verb "to finish" and *re*-, meaning again. This word is often seen in the phrase "refined manners," which describes someone with highly polished manners.

relinquish *(v.)* riˈliNGkwiSH
To give up.

*When she suddenly became very sick, she was forced to **relinquish** her role as CEO.*

From Old French for "to leave." *Renounce* is a synonym for *relinquish*.

ramshackle *(adj.)* ramˌSHakəl
Run-down, describing a building or structure.

*Once a warren of **ramshackle** buildings, the west end of town has recently been gentrified.*

Likely from Scottish dialect, this originally meant "to loot a home." *Dilapidated* is a synonym.

revert *(v.)* riˈvərt
To change back to an earlier state.

resilient *(adj.)* riˈzilyənt
Able to bounce back from hardships.

retribution *(n.)*
retrəˈbyōoSHən
Deserved punishment.

ACTIVITY 196

Mark "S" if the meanings of the two words are similar, "O" if they are opposite, or "D" if they are different:

1. revert and relinquish _____

2. refine and spoil _____

3. retribution and distribution _____

4. ramshackle and dilapidated _____

Words Beginning with S

stringent *(adj.)* strinjənt
Extremely strict, usually referring to rules.

*The rules in the boarding school were highly **stringent**, and students were not allowed to make noise after 8 p.m. nor leave their rooms after this time unless accompanied by an adult.*

This word comes from the Latin for "becoming tight." Though the word *astringent* has the same root, it refers to something that is bitter tasting.

soporific *(adj.)* ˌsäpəˈrifik
Causing sleep.

*The movie had great actors, but the **soporific** scenes lulled the audience to sleep.*

From the Latin for "to sleep." This word can also describe something that is boring and tedious.

spurious *(adj.)* spyo͞orēəs
Fake, counterfeit.

*The reports that the city had fallen to the enemy were **spurious**.*

This comes from the Latin for "false." *Bogus* and *fraudulent* are two synonyms.

sequential *(adj.)*
siˈkwenCHəl
Following in order.

stark *(adj.)* stärk
Standing out strongly.

spurn *(v.)* spərn
To reject.

specious *(adj.)* spēSHəs
Attractive at first glance but not so upon closer examination.

ACTIVITY 197

Write the word that completes each sentence:

1. There was a _____ difference between his freshman GPA (when he was on probation) and his senior GPA (when he was on the dean's list).

2. He _____ any clothes that he thought were outmoded, preferring the latest trends.

3. Over-the-counter flu medicines tend to be _____, helping many fall asleep more easily.

Provide the word for the given definition:

4. fake = _____

5. attractive at first glance but not so upon closer examination = _____

6. extremely strict = _____

Words Beginning with T

tantamount *(adj.)* ˈtantəˌmount
Equivalent to.

*His statement that he couldn't remember where he was on the night of the crime was, at least for the prosecution, **tantamount** to an admission of guilt.*

From the Italian for "amounting to the same." Two phrases that are similar to *tantamount* are "on par with" and "much the same as."

taut *(adj.)* tôt
Tight and tense.

*The movie scenes were **taut**, not a single moment seemed unnecessary.*

This word might be related to "tough." *Taut* is often used to describe muscles that are very tight and lean (think of an Olympic sprinter).

travesty *(n.)* travistē
An absurd, grossly inferior imitation of the real thing.

*His recent novel was a **travesty**: There was no real plot, characters were left undeveloped, and there was no discernible conclusion.*

Comes from the Italian for "disguised in ridiculous clothing." This word should not be confused with *tragedy*.

triage *(n.)* trēˈäZH
A process by which the most serious cases are identified and treated first.

tempest *(n.)* Tempest
A strong wind.

titillate *(v.)* titlˌāt
To excite.

ACTIVITY 198

Fill in the missing letters to complete the word:

1. t_____t (3 possible words)

2. t___ate

3. tr___ge

4. t____sty

Words Beginning with U

unanimous (*adj.*) yo͞oˈnanəməs
Agreed on by all.

*The pollution was so obvious that the city board's **unanimous** vote to close down the factory surprised nobody.*

From the Latin for "one mind." *Unanimous* indicates 100 percent agreement among all parties involved. Even if 98 out of 100 agree on something, this is still not unanimous.

undulate (*v.*) ənjəˌlāt
To move in a wavelike manner.

*The young recruits formed a sea of **undulating** bodies as they crawled under rows of barbed wire fences.*

Comes from the Latin for "a wave." This word can also be used to describe the rise and fall of sound.

unctuous (*adj.*) əng(k)CHo͞oəs
Excessively flattering.

*The car salesman wore an **unctuous** smile as he said, "Mrs. Jones, you would look amazing in that red sports car!"*

This word comes from the Latin for "to anoint with oil." This word can also describe something that is oily and soapy, though this usage is not as common.

unassuming (*adj.*) ənəˈso͞omiNG
Modest.

usher (*v.*) əSHər
To bring about or cause to happen.

utilitarian (*adj.*) yo͞oˌtiliˈte(ə)rēən
Serving a useful function but not necessarily attractive.

ululate (*v.*) ˈəlyəˌlāt
To howl like a wolf.

ACTIVITY 199

Write the word that completes each sentence:

1. Always dressed in sweatpants and a baseball cap, he looked _____, though he was worth over a billion dollars.

2. The Internet has _____ in changes to the social landscape that 20 years ago would have been the stuff of science fiction.

3. With its many peaks and valleys, the landscape _____ as far as the eye could sea.

4. The building was _____, providing hundreds of offices but about as nondescript as a prison cell block.

5. Kendrick had trouble making friends because he was too _____; people did not believe he was sincere and hence did not trust him.

Words Beginning with V

vacuous *(adj.)* vakyəwəs
Lacking intelligence and the ability to generate interesting thoughts.

*As the summer went on and there was little to do beyond watch television, the two brothers took on an increasingly **vacuous** look.*

This word comes from the Latin for "empty." This word has two acceptable noun forms, either *vacuity* or *vacuousness*.

vaunt *(v.)* vônt
To boast continually.

*The much-**vaunted** sports area turned out to have uncomfortable seats, overpriced food, and narrow entryways.*

From the Latin for "vain and empty." This verb is most often used in its participle form—*vaunted*—to describe something that is continuously boasted about (see example sentence).

vehement *(adj.)* vēəmənt
Passionate and intense.

*His **vehement** argument for subsidized cafeteria lunches revealed how deeply he felt about the issue.*

This word is from the Latin for "violent." The noun form of this word is *vehemence*.

valiant *(adj.)* valyənt
Brave, daring.

vouch *(n.)* vouCH
To speak in favor of someone or something based on one's experience.

vernacular *(n.)*
vərˈnakyələr
A specific way of speaking to a particular group or region.

vignette *(n.)* vinˈyet
A short sketch, a brief but detailed description.

ACTIVITY 200

Match the word with its meaning:

1. brave, daring _____
2. way of speaking to a specific area _____
3. to attest that someone is of a certain character _____
4. intensely passionate _____
5. short sketch _____
6. boast _____

a. vernacular
b. vignette
c. vaunt
d. vehement
e. vouch
f. valiant

FURTHER RESOURCES

Vocabulary.com

This site provides not just definitions but also the context in which words are used, ultimately offering a much fuller sense of what words mean and how to use them in the real world.

Quizlet.com

Flashcards are a great way to get words to stick. With Quizlet you can make as many flashcards as you want online, and then study on the go.

theFreeDictionary.com

Easy-to-digest definitions along with a daily word-matching game make this a useful site to visit.

Dictionary.com

This is a good source for concise definitions.

Memrise.com

This site contains roots galore, as well as effective ways to make words stick in your long-term memory.

books.google.com/ngrams

Enter a word into the Google Books Ngram Viewer to see how common it is and how its usage has changed over time. In addition to being mildly addictive, this site will give you a good sense of just how widely used certain words are and, by extension, which ones should be a part of your vocabulary.

Merriam-Webster.com

This is a good source for definitions and also offers plenty of vocabulary games and an interesting blog.

***Word Power Made Easy* by Norman Lewis**

This classic is similar to this book in that it groups words according to families and also provides short activities.

***Barron's 1100 Words You Need to Know* by Murray Bromberg and Melvin Gordon**

This book is a great place to learn words through context instead of merely parroting definitions. Plenty of activities provide examples of how words appear in published sources.

Magoosh.com

Magoosh's GRE vocabulary blog and Vocabulary Wednesday videos are a great place to get descriptions of the more difficult words likely to appear on the GRE.

ANSWER KEY

☐ ACTIVITY 1
1. precipitate
2. predilection
3. R
4. NR

☐ ACTIVITY 2
1. precocious
2. preclude
3. precedent
4. S
5. NR
6. NR

☐ ACTIVITY 3
1. f
2. e
3. a
4. d
5. b
6. c

☐ ACTIVITY 4
1. spartan
2. platonic
3. thespian
4. hector
5. nemesis
6. juggernaut
7. pyrrhic
8. maudlin

☐ ACTIVITY 5
1. arriviste = parvenu
2. insouciant = nonchalant
3. subterfuge = chicanery
4. demur
5. chicanery

☐ ACTIVITY 6
1. sangfroid
2. rapport
3. passé
4. gauche
5. cache
6. raconteur

☐ ACTIVITY 7
1. liaison
2. sans
3. droll
4. envoy
5. filial

☐ ACTIVITY 8
1. e
2. a
3. g
4. f
5. b
6. c
7. d

☐ ACTIVITY 9

1. poltergeist
2. verboten
3. zeitgeist
4. schadenfreude
5. bildungsroman
6. kaput
7. kitsch
8. doppelganger

☐ ACTIVITY 10

1. archipelago
2. citadel
3. pastiche
4. salvo
5. located along the coast
6. complicated situation
7. an exaggerated imitation

☐ ACTIVITY 11

1. dilettante, cognoscenti
2. ruffian, bravado
3. the highly educated people in a society
4. a declaration describing the aims of a group

☐ ACTIVITY 12

1. e
2. a
3. f
4. b
5. c
6. d
7. g

☐ ACTIVITY 13

1. O
2. S
3. S (not exactly the same, though)
4. D

☐ ACTIVITY 14

1. predicament
2. prepossessing
3. punctilious
4. restive
5. sedulous
6. peruse
7. equivocate

☐ ACTIVITY 15

1. burnish
2. redress
3. remiss
4. quiescent
5. intemperate
6. gratuitous

☐ ACTIVITY 16

1. rambunctious
2. raucous
3. obstreperous
4. murmur
5. susurrus
6. hubbub

☐ ACTIVITY 17

1. O
2. S
3. D

ACTIVITY 18
1. verbose
2. palaver
3. mince
4. hedge
5. taciturn

ACTIVITY 19
1. cornucopia
2. surfeit
3. legion
4. myriad
5. plethora

ACTIVITY 20
1. extraneous, superfluous
2. modicum
3. iota
4. wanting
5. dearth, paucity

ACTIVITY 21
1. didactic
2. repudiate
3. doctrinaire
4. adamant
5. assertive

ACTIVITY 22
1. T
2. F
3. T
4. T

ACTIVITY 23
1. d
2. e
3. a
4. b
5. c

ACTIVITY 24
1. lionize
2. reproach
3. laud
4. hail
5. deprecate
6. approbative

ACTIVITY 25
1. pejorative
2. venerate
3. belittle
4. kudos
5. commend

ACTIVITY 26
1. O
2. O
3. O
4. S

ACTIVITY 27
1. industrious, assiduous
2. bustle
3. celerity, dispatch
4. lackadaisical

ACTIVITY 28
1. tautology
2. barbarism
3. archaic
4. eponymous
5. palindromes
6. portmanteau

ACTIVITY 29
1. S
2. D
3. D
4. D

ACTIVITY 30

1. pedantic, erudite
2. eminent
3. pedagogue
4. collegial
5. benighted

ACTIVITY 31

1. R
2. NR
3. NR
4. NR

ACTIVITY 32

1. O
2. S
3. D
4. D

ACTIVITY 33

1. philistine
2. base, ignoble, contemptible
3. vulgar
4. uncultivated

ACTIVITY 34

1. virtuoso
2. forte
3. mellifluous
4. crescendo
5. coda

ACTIVITY 35

1. badger
2. ape
3. crow
4. slothful
5. mulish

ACTIVITY 36

1. elephantine
2. apian
3. simian
4. vulpine
5. asinine
6. avian
7. ursine
8. bovine

ACTIVITY 37

1. agnostic
2. sacrilege
3. apostate
4. iconoclast

ACTIVITY 38

1. NR
2. NR
3. NR
4. NR

ACTIVITY 39

1. expurgate
2. exude
3. expunge
4. extenuate
5. exonerate
6. execrate

ACTIVITY 40

1. discrete
2. venal
3. effect
4. affected

☐ ACTIVITY 41

1. complaisant
2. censured
3. emigrating
4. censor
5. complacent
6. elude

☐ ACTIVITY 42

1. foundered
2. tortuous
3. proscribed
4. elicit
5. torturous

☐ ACTIVITY 43

1. S
2. S
3. NR

☐ ACTIVITY 44

1. raillery
2. besmirch
3. impugn
4. vilify, traduce

☐ ACTIVITY 45

1. c
2. d
3. b
4. e
5. a

☐ ACTIVITY 46

1. propitiate
2. contentious
3. jingoist
4. implacable
5. truculent
6. conciliatory

☐ ACTIVITY 47

1. S
2. NR
3. R (these imply different degrees of fear)

☐ ACTIVITY 48

1. synergy
2. schism
3. hierarchy
4. R (both describe groups but aren't quite the same thing)
5. S
6. S

☐ ACTIVITY 49

1. tyrant
2. despot
3. autocratic
4. subjugate

☐ ACTIVITY 50

1. S
2. O
3. S

☐ ACTIVITY 51

1. S
2. R
3. NR
4. vicissitude
5. tribulations, travail

☐ ACTIVITY 52

1. persnickety, fastidious; quibble
2. perfunctory
3. slipshod
4. scrutinize
5. cursory

ACTIVITY 53

1. moribund
2. chrysalis
3. senile
4. callow, fledgling
5. geriatric
6. juvenile

ACTIVITY 54

1. unassailable
2. riposte
3. forensics
4. parry
5. maintain

ACTIVITY 55

1. extrovert
2. debauchery
3. inebriated
4. retiring
5. affable

ACTIVITY 56

1. bucolic, rustic, pastoral
2. verdant
3. lush
4. barren
5. idyllic

ACTIVITY 57

1. D
2. S
3. S
4. O

ACTIVITY 58

1. D
2. D
3. S
4. S

ACTIVITY 59

1. junta, usurp
2. cataclysmic
3. turmoil
4. concord

ACTIVITY 60

1. g
2. f
3. d
4. h
5. b
6. a
7. c
8. e

ACTIVITY 61

1. f
2. e
3. c
4. h
5. g
6. d
7. b
8. a

ACTIVITY 62

1. g
2. f
3. b
4. h
5. d
6. c
7. e
8. a

ACTIVITY 63

1. f
2. c
3. a
4. e
5. b
6. d

ACTIVITY 64

1. ambivalent
2. saturnine, morose
3. dour
4. elated
5. blithe

ACTIVITY 65

1. crepuscular
2. antediluvian
3. fin-de-siècle
4. bimonthly
5. semimonthly
6. fortnight

ACTIVITY 66

1. briny
2. acrid
3. toothsome
4. insipid
5. palatable
6. succulent

ACTIVITY 67

1. effervescent
2. buoyant
3. avocation, diversion
4. stultifying
5. ennui

ACTIVITY 68

1. S
2. D
3. D
4. D

ACTIVITY 69

1. protean
2. fatuous
3. panache
4. buttressed
5. hapless
6. garish

ACTIVITY 70

1. e
2. c
3. a
4. g
5. b
6. f
7. d

ACTIVITY 71

1. ruddy
2. purple
3. cynosure
4. blackball
5. flamboyant

ACTIVITY 72

1. parsimonious, miserly, frugal
2. economical
3. munificence, largesse
4. magnanimous

☐ ACTIVITY 73

1. sybarite, hedonist
2. profligate, prodigal
3. profligate
4. spendthrift

☐ ACTIVITY 74

1. NR
2. S
3. NR
4. NR

☐ ACTIVITY 75

1. elysian
2. dionysian
3. apollonian
4. narcissist
5. chimera
6. herculean

☐ ACTIVITY 76

1. cosmogony
2. sublime
3. numinous
4. theodicy
5. cherub
6. seraphic

☐ ACTIVITY 77

1. T
2. F
3. T
4. F

☐ ACTIVITY 78

1. S
2. D
3. D
4. D

☐ ACTIVITY 79

1. polymath
2. maven
3. tyro
4. savant
5. novice
6. greenhorn

☐ ACTIVITY 80

1. opulent, lavish
2. avarice, cupidity
3. destitute, affluent
4. lavish, opulent

☐ ACTIVITY 81

1. f
2. e
3. d
4. a
5. b
6. c

☐ ACTIVITY 82

1. f
2. g
3. a
4. b
5. c
6. e
7. d

☐ ACTIVITY 83

1. S
2. O
3. S
4. O

ACTIVITY 84

1. leviathan
2. pestilence
3. atonement
4. advent

ACTIVITY 85

1. c
2. f
3. d
4. b
5. a
6. e

ACTIVITY 86

1. S
2. S
3. D (*dirge* is a sad song, whereas a *lament* doesn't take song form)

ACTIVITY 87

1. S
2. D
3. D
4. snubbed
5. fanfare

ACTIVITY 88

1. S
2. D
3. D

ACTIVITY 89

1. irreproachable
2. incorruptible
3. turpitude
4. scrupulous
5. ruthless

ACTIVITY 90

1. O
2. D
3. D
4. S

ACTIVITY 91

1. ponderous
2. confound
3. nonplussed
4. histrionic
5. contrite

ACTIVITY 92

1. shtick
2. schmaltzy
3. kibitz
4. klutz
5. chutzpah
6. kvetch

ACTIVITY 93

1. clairvoyant
2. berserk
3. maelstrom
4. bazaar
5. mecca
6. hegira

ACTIVITY 94

1. mundane
2. penultimate
3. abysmal
4. mediocre
5. cardinal
6. nonpareil

ACTIVITY 95

1. irrefutable
2. empirical
3. centripetal
4. fulcrum
5. hypothesize
6. catalyst

ACTIVITY 96

1. D
2. D
3. O
4. D (*ubiquitous* does not have a negative connotation)

ACTIVITY 97

1. D
2. D
3. S
4. D

ACTIVITY 98

1. O
2. D
3. D

ACTIVITY 99

1. marauding
2. annex, cede
3. accord
4. armistice
5. entente

ACTIVITY 100

1. c
2. f
3. d
4. a
5. b
6. e

ACTIVITY 101

1. lambaste
2. rail
3. aspersion
4. invidious
5. vituperative
6. inveigh

ACTIVITY 102

1. S
2. O
3. O

ACTIVITY 103

1. aphorism, maxim
2. dictum
3. precept
4. bromide, cliché, platitude

ACTIVITY 104

1. exacerbate, escalate
2. assuage
3. truncated
4. abated
5. cessation

ACTIVITY 105

1. selfless, altruistic
2. self-effacing
3. modest
4. self-deprecating
5. self-aggrandizing

ACTIVITY 106

1. woe
2. vie
3. imp
4. mar
5. eke
6. ire
7. nub

ACTIVITY 107

1. moil
2. foil
3. pith
4. curt
5. deft
6. crux
7. carp
8. char

ACTIVITY 108

1. prognostication
2. disenchantment
3. commensurate
4. indefatigable
5. infinitesimal

ACTIVITY 109

1. D
2. S
3. D
4. O

ACTIVITY 110

1. fracas
2. furor
3. détente
4. ado
5. rift
6. melee
7. fiasco

ACTIVITY 111

1. trite
2. hackneyed
3. prosaic
4. banal
5. quotidian
6. pedestrian

ACTIVITY 112

1. F
2. F
3. T
4. F
5. T

ACTIVITY 113

1. O
2. S
3. O
4. D (*coaxing* involves flattery)

ACTIVITY 114

1. S
2. S
3. O
4. S

ACTIVITY 115

1. presumption
2. conjecture, speculation
3. submit
4. posit
5. aver
6. presumption

ACTIVITY 116

1. D
2. S
3. D
4. O

ACTIVITY 117

1. wrath
2. peeved, piqued
3. irate, incensed
4. disgruntled

ACTIVITY 118

1. intrepid
2. plucky
3. valorous
4. redoubtable
5. pusillanimous
6. craven

ACTIVITY 119

1. S
2. R (*promulgate* means "to announce changes" but not to actually put them into practice, the way *enact* does)
3. S
4. S

ACTIVITY 120

1. astute, shrewd, acute
2. obtuse
3. bailiwick, niche

ACTIVITY 121

1. benign, benevolent
2. benign
3. beneficiary
4. benediction
5. beneficial

ACTIVITY 122

1. malice
2. malign
3. maleficent
4. malapropism
5. malodorous
6. malaria
7. malady
8. malfeasance

ACTIVITY 123

1. phonetic
2. francophone
3. homophone
4. cacophony
5. anglophone
6. phoneme

ACTIVITY 124

1. eulogy
2. euphony
3. eureka
4. euphemism
5. euthanasia

ACTIVITY 125

1. anthropogenic
2. anthropology
3. Anthropocene
4. anthropocentric
5. anthropomorphism

ACTIVITY 126

1. circumambulate
2. circumscribe
3. circumlocution
4. circumference
5. circumvent

ACTIVITY 127

1. theocracy
2. democracy
3. aristocracy
4. plutocracy
5. bureaucracy
6. gerontocracy

ACTIVITY 128

1. diurnal
2. dichotomy
3. diverge
4. dissect
5. dilate
6. diverse

ACTIVITY 129

1. diadem
2. diorama
3. diapason
4. dialogue
5. diameter
6. diagnosis

ACTIVITY 130

1. epistolary
2. epithet
3. epigram
4. epitaph
5. epigraph
6. epidemic
7. epitome

ACTIVITY 131

1. a
2. f
3. g
4. b
5. c
6. d
7. e

ACTIVITY 132

1. exploit
2. expend
3. explicating
4. expedient
5. expeditious
6. exhume
7. exorcise

ACTIVITY 133

1. c
2. b
3. a
4. e
5. f
6. d
7. g

ACTIVITY 134

1. imbibe
2. impart
3. impair
4. impeach
5. imbue

ACTIVITY 135

1. implore
2. impel
3. impoverished
4. imponderable

ACTIVITY 136

1. f
2. d
3. a
4. e
5. b
6. c
7. g

ACTIVITY 137

1. incarcerated
2. incipient
3. incinerated
4. incite
5. inclement
6. incentivize

ACTIVITY 138

1. incorrigible
2. indiscriminate
3. incredulous
4. incontrovertible

ACTIVITY 139

1. e
2. f
3. d
4. b
5. c
6. a

ACTIVITY 140

1. g
2. e
3. f
4. c
5. d
6. b
7. a

ACTIVITY 141

1. interject
2. interrogated
3. intercede
4. interdict
5. interim
6. intersperse

ACTIVITY 142

1. f
2. e
3. b
4. c
5. d
6. a

ACTIVITY 143

1. f
2. c
3. b
4. g
5. e
6. d
7. a

ACTIVITY 144

1. e
2. f
3. g
4. b
5. c
6. a
7. d

ACTIVITY 145

1. fractured
2. fragile
3. fragments
4. refractory
5. fractious

ACTIVITY 146

1. belligerent, bellicose
2. casus belli
3. antebellum
4. belle
5. bellow

ACTIVITY 147

1. a
2. e
3. d
4. c
5. b

ACTIVITY 148

1. reconnoitered, reconnaissance
2. precognition
3. incognito
4. cognitive

ACTIVITY 149

1. diminution
2. minatory
3. minute
4. prominent
5. imminent

ACTIVITY 150

1. e
2. f
3. g
4. b
5. c
6. d
7. a

ACTIVITY 151

1. a
2. b
3. c
4. d
5. f
6. e

ACTIVITY 152

1. pandemic
2. panoply
3. panegyrics
4. panacea
5. pandemonium

ACTIVITY 153

1. e
2. a
3. f
4. b
5. d
6. c

ACTIVITY 154

1. periscope
2. periodontal
3. perigee
4. perihelion
5. periphrastic
6. peripheral

ACTIVITY 155

1. conscript
2. inscribe
3. scribe
4. ascribe
5. subscribe

ACTIVITY 156

1. g
2. c
3. b
4. a
5. f
6. d
7. e

ACTIVITY 157

1. prolix
2. propagated
3. provenance
4. providential
5. protuberance
6. protracted
7. procrastinate

ACTIVITY 158

1. poignant
2. compunction
3. punctilio
4. punctuate

ACTIVITY 159

1. undisputable
2. putative
3. impute
4. dispute
5. disreputable

ACTIVITY 160

1. acquisition
2. inquisition
3. requisition
4. prerequisite
5. perquisite

ACTIVITY 161

1. supererogatory
2. derogate
3. prerogative
4. roguish
5. surrogate
6. arrogate

ACTIVITY 162

1. subsequent
2. sequestered
3. inconsequential
4. obsequious

ACTIVITY 163

1. eclectic
2. ecstatic
3. anecdote
4. eccentric

ACTIVITY 164

1. aficionado
2. abridge
3. ameliorate
4. abut
5. abet

ACTIVITY 165

1. anomalous, atypical
2. amnesty
3. atrophy
4. atheist
5. aphasia

ACTIVITY 166

1. solicitous
2. cite
3. resuscitate
4. unsolicited

ACTIVITY 167

1. d
2. b
3. a
4. c
5. f
6. e

ACTIVITY 168

1. contumacious
2. conjugal
3. contiguous
4. congeal
5. connote

ACTIVITY 169

1. devolving
2. debunked
3. detritus
4. decipher
5. decadent
6. denouement

ACTIVITY 170

1. f
2. a
3. d
4. c
5. b
6. e

ACTIVITY 171

1. f
2. b
3. c
4. d
5. a
6. e

ACTIVITY 172

1. enormity
2. enunciate
3. ineluctable
4. elocution
5. evocative

ACTIVITY 173

1. f
2. d
3. e
4. c
5. a
6. b

ACTIVITY 174

1. f
2. e
3. a
4. c
5. b
6. d

ACTIVITY 175

1. genocide
2. genesis
3. indigenous
4. genealogy
5. carcinogenic

ACTIVITY 176

1. b
2. e
3. c
4. a
5. d

ACTIVITY 177

1. d
2. c
3. b
4. f
5. a
6. e

ACTIVITY 178

1. navigate
2. exigent
3. unmitigated
4. ambiguous
5. mitigate
6. castigate

ACTIVITY 179

1. appendix
2. impending
3. pending
4. compendious
5. expenditure

ACTIVITY 180

1. regnant
2. regiment
3. regicide
4. regalia
5. regent
6. regal

ACTIVITY 181

1. admonished
2. agrarian
3. adulated
4. ascertain
5. antiquated

ACTIVITY 182

1. e
2. d
3. a
4. b
5. c
6. f

ACTIVITY 183

1. commiserated
2. clambering
3. catatonic
4. to go about making revelry
5. ill-tempered
6. to conspire

ACTIVITY 184

1. e
2. a
3. f
4. d
5. g
6. b
7. c

ACTIVITY 185

1. espouse
2. endowed
3. evident
4. entertain
5. eradicate

ACTIVITY 186

1. fickle
2. feral
3. foisted
4. to waste
5. delicate outlines or tracings
6. to decorate with garlands

ACTIVITY 187

1. f
2. c
3. a
4. g
5. b
6. e
7. d

ACTIVITY 188

1. g
2. f
3. e
4. d
5. c
6. b
7. a

ACTIVITY 189

1. impetus
2. imprint
3. intuition
4. idiom
5. impervious

ACTIVITY 190

1. c
2. b
3. e
4. a
5. f
6. d

ACTIVITY 191

1. mull
2. meander
3. maim
4. myopic
5. mirth

ACTIVITY 192

1. nimble
2. natter
3. nary
4. noisome
5. nadir
6. negligible

ACTIVITY 193

1. c
2. g
3. d
4. f
5. e
6. a
7. b

ACTIVITY 194

1. pilfer
2. preempt
3. pander
4. penchant
5. prevaricate
6. peddle
7. perpetuate

ACTIVITY 195

1. b
2. c
3. e
4. d
5. f
6. a

ACTIVITY 196

1. D
2. O
3. D
4. S

ACTIVITY 197

1. stark
2. spurned
3. soporific
4. spurious
5. specious
6. stringent

ACTIVITY 198

1. taut, tempest, tantamount
2. titillate
3. triage
4. travesty

ACTIVITY 199

1. unassuming
2. ushered
3. undulated
4. utilitarian
5. unctuous

ACTIVITY 200

1. f
2. a
3. e
4. d
5. b
6. c

INDEX